بسم الله الرحمن الرحيم

A Practical Guide
to
Spiritual Wayfaring

A Practical Guide to Spiritual Wayfaring

SHAYKH-UL-ISLAM
DR MUHAMMAD TAHIR-UL-QADRI

Author: Dr Muhammad Tahir-ul-Qadri

Published by
Minhaj-ul-Quran Publications
30 Brindley Road
Manchester
M16 9HQ

All proceeds from the books, literature and audio-visual media (all multimedia) delivered by Dr Muhammad Tahir-ul-Qadri are entirely donated to Minhaj-ul-Quran International (MQI).

Translation and Editorial Team
Ayub Anwar and Jawed Iqbal Tahiri

Acknowledgement
Minhaj Women League Midlands Zone (UK)
Muhammad Qasim Khan (UK)

ISBN: 978–1–913553-45-6

www.minhaj.org | www.minhajuk.org
www.minhajpublications.com

First published November 2022

Printed in the UK

بِسْمِ اللَّهِ الرَّحْمَٰنِ الرَّحِيمِ

In the name of God, Most Compassionate, Ever-Merciful

﴿وَنَفْسٍ وَمَا سَوَّىٰهَا ۝٧ فَأَلْهَمَهَا فُجُورَهَا وَتَقْوَىٰهَا ۝٨ قَدْ أَفْلَحَ
مَن زَكَّىٰهَا ۝٩ وَقَدْ خَابَ مَن دَسَّىٰهَا ۝١٠﴾

And by the human soul and by the One Who provided it with an all-dimensional poise, proportion and perfection. Then He inspired it with (discrimination between) vice and virtue. Indeed, the one who purifies his (ill-commanding) self (from all vain and vicious desires and cultivates in it virtue and piousness) succeeds, but the one who corrupts himself (in sins and suppresses virtue) is doomed indeed. [Qur'ān 91:7–10]

Saying of the Holy Prophet ﷺ

«أَلَا وَإِنَّ فِي الْجَسَدِ مُضْغَةً، إِذَا صَلَحَتْ صَلَحَ الْجَسَدُ كُلُّهُ، وَإِذَا فَسَدَتْ فَسَدَ الْجَسَدُ كُلُّهُ، أَلَا وَهِيَ الْقَلْبُ.»

Beware! Verily, there is a piece of flesh in the body, if it is sound, the whole body is sound, and if it is corrupt, the whole body is corrupt – verily, it is the heart. [al-Bukhārī and Muslim]

Shaykh-ul-Islam Dr Muhammad Tahir-ul-Qadri

Shaykh-ul-Islam Dr Muhammad Tahir-ul-Qadri was born in 1951 in the city of Jhang, Pakistan, hailing from a family of Islamic saints, scholars and teachers. His formal religious education was initiated in Medina at the age of 12 in Madrasa al-ʿUlūm al-Sharʿiyya, a traditional school situated in the blessed house of the Companion of the Prophet Muhammad ﷺ, Abū Ayyūb al-Anṣārī ؓ. He completed the traditional studies of classical and Arabic sciences under the tutelage of his father and other eminent scholars of the time. He continued to travel around the Islamic world in pursuit of sacred knowledge, and studied under many famous scholars of Mecca, Medina, Syria, Baghdad, Lebanon, the Maghreb, India and Pakistan, and received around five hundred authorities and chains of transmission from them in hadith and classical Islamic and spiritual sciences. Amongst them is an unprecedented, unique and highly honoured chain of authority which connects him, through five teachers, to al-Ghawth al-Aʿẓam al-Shaykh ʿAbd al-Qādir al-Jīlānī (of Baghdad), al-Shaykh al-Akbar Muḥyī al-Dīn b. ʿArabī—the author of *al-Futūḥāt al-Makkiyya*—(Damascus) and al-Ḥāfiẓ Ibn Ḥajar al-ʿAsqalānī, the great hadith authority of Egypt. Through another chain he is linked to Imam Yūsuf b. Ismāʿīl al-Nabhānī directly via only one teacher. His chains of transmission are published in two of his *thabts* (detailed lists): *al-Jawāhir al-Bāhira fī al-Asānīd al-Ṭāhira* and *al-Subul al Wahabiyya fī al-Asānīd al-Dhahabiyya*.

In the academic sphere, Dr Qadri received a First Class Honours Degree from the University of the Punjab in 1970. After earning his MA in Islamic studies with University Gold Medal in 1972 and achieving his LLB in 1974, Dr Qadri began to practise law in the district courts of Jhang. He moved to Lahore in 1978 and joined the University of the Punjab as a lecturer in law and completed his doctorate in Islamic Law. He was later appointed as a professor of Islamic Law and was head of the department of Islamic legislation for LLM.

Dr Qadri was also a jurist advisor to the Federal Shariat Court and Appellate Shariah Bench of the Supreme Court of Pakistan and advisor on the development of Islamic Curricula to the Federal Ministry of Education. Within a short span of time, Dr Qadri emerged as one of the Pakistan's leading Islamic jurists and scholars and one of the world's most renowned and leading authorities on Islam. A prolific author, researcher and orator, Dr Qadri has written around one thousand books, of which about six hundred have been published; and has delivered over six thousand lectures (in Urdu, English and Arabic) on a wide range of subjects.

In 2010, Shaykh-ul-Islam Dr Muhammad Tahir-ul-Qadri issued his historic and world-renowned fatwa on the critical matter of suicide bombings and terrorism carried out in the name of Islam. It has been regarded as a significant and historic step, the first time that such an explicit and unequivocal decree against the perpetrators of terror has been broadcast so widely. The original fatwa written in Urdu comprises 600 pages of research and references from the Qur'ān, hadith, the opinions of the Companions ﷺ, and the widely accepted classical texts of Islamic scholarship. This historic work has been published in English, Arabic, Norwegian, French, Bahasa Indonesia, Hindi and Sindhi, while translation in Danish, Spanish, Malayalam, Persian, Turkish and other major languages is also in process. The Islamic Research Academy of Jamia al-Azhar Egypt wrote a detailed description of the fatwa and verified its contents. It gained worldwide media attention and acclaim as an indispensable tool in the intellectual and ideological struggle against violent extremism.

In 2018, Shaykh-ul-Islam Dr Muhammad Tahir-ul-Qadri launched his magnanimous *Qur'ānic Encyclopædia*. This encyclopaedia is the cumulation of his fifty-year long effort in studying the Qur'ān and it comprises eight volumes consisting of around five thousand subjects. The subjects have been worded according to contemporary requirements and needs. From the encyclopaedia's unique features, one will find modern, scientific and philosophic subjects addressed. It is impossible to encompass all the subjects and topics that are discussed in the Qur'ān. However, the *Qur'ānic Encyclopædia*, with its approximately five thousand subjects, is exhaustive and comprehensive in terms of contemporary needs and requirements. Last three volumes contain a comprehensive index of Qur'ānic words. This index will facilitate in accessing the shoreless oceans of meaning in the Qur'ān.

Also Dr Qadri is the founder and head of Minhaj-ul-Quran International (MQI), an organization with branches and centres in more than ninety countries around the globe; he is the chairman of the Board of Governors of Minhaj University Lahore (MUL), which is chartered by the Government of Pakistan; he is the founder of Minhaj Education Society (MES), which has established more than 600 schools and colleges in Pakistan; and he is the chairman of Minhaj Welfare Foundation (MWF), an organization involved in humanitarian and social welfare activities globally.

Dr Qadri has spent his life, and especially the last decade, in an indefatigable effort to counter religious extremism and promote peace and harmony between communities. His painstaking research into the Qur'ān, hadith and classical Islamic authorities has resulted in landmark works, many published, and others soon to be published, demonstrating Islam as a religion that not only safeguards human rights, but promotes peace, tolerance and socioeconomic progress. He has travelled extensively to lecture at the invitation of government and non-government institutions, and has organized and took part in international conferences in order to promote peace. He has arrayed spiritual and educational training programmes across the Western world with a focus on addressing the roots of religious extremism. He is recognised for his commitment to interfaith dialogue, with over 12,000 people attending his Peace for Humanity Conference in 2011, probably the largest interfaith gathering ever held in the UK, and which announced the London Declaration, a charter for world peace, signed online by a quarter of a million people. He has been politically active in his native Pakistan, organizing massive pro-democracy and anti-corruption demonstrations. When not travelling, he is based in Canada, busy in his research activities and producing vital works of Islamic scholarship relevant to Muslims in this day and age.

Formulaic Arabic Expressions

(*Subḥānahū wa taʿālā*)—an invocation to describe the Glory of Almighty Allah: 'the Exalted and Sublime'

ﷺ (*Ṣalla-Llāhu ʿalayhi wa ālihī wa sallam*)—an invocation of God's blessings and peace upon the Prophet Muhammad ﷺ and his family: 'God's blessings and peace be upon him and his family'

(*ʿAlayhiʾs-salām*)—an invocation of God's blessings and peace upon a Prophet or an angel or a pious person: 'May peace be upon him'

(*ʿAlayhaʾs-salām*)—an invocation of God's blessings and peace upon a Prophet's mother, wife, daughter and other pious woman: 'May peace be upon her'

(*ʿAlayhimaʾs-salām*)—an invocation of God's blessings and peace upon two Prophets or two angels or two pious persons: 'May peace be upon both of them'

(*ʿAlayhimuʾs-salām*)—an invocation of God's blessings and peace upon three or more Prophets: 'May peace be upon them'

(*Raḍiya-Llāhu ʿanhu*)—an invocation of God's pleasure with a male Companion of the Prophet Muhammad ﷺ: 'May God be pleased with him'

(*Raḍiya-Llāhu ʿanhā*)—an invocation of God's pleasure with a female Companion of the Prophet Muhammad ﷺ: 'May God be pleased with her'

(*Raḍiya-Llāhu ʿanhumā*)—an invocation of God's pleasure with two Companions of the Prophet Muhammad ﷺ: 'May God be pleased with both of them'

(*Raḍiya-Llāhu ʿanhum*)—an invocation of God's pleasure with more than two Companions of the Prophet Muhammad ﷺ: 'May God be pleased with them'

Transliteration Key

ا/ آ/ ى	ā	غ	gh
ب	b	ف	f
ت	t	ق	q
ث	th	ك	k
ج	j	ل	l
ح	ḥ	م	m
خ	kh	ن	n
د	d	هـ/ ه	h
ذ	dh	و	ū/w
ر	r	ي	y/ī
ز	z	ة	a
س	s	ء	ʾ
ش	sh	أ	a
ص	ṣ	إ	i
ض	ḍ		
ط	ṭ	ـَ	a
ظ	ẓ	ـِ	i
ع	ʿ	ـُ	u

CONTENT

Chapter 1

SUFISM IN ISLAMIC HISTORY 1

1.1 A Brief Historical View on Sufism in Muslim Lands 3

1.2 The Two Dimensions of Islam and the Two Promises for its Preservation 8

Chapter 2

PRINCIPLES OF SUFISM IN THE ERA OF THE HOLY PROPHET ﷺ AND THE COMPANIONS 13

2.1 Principles of Sufism from the Sunna 14

2.1.1 Wearing the Woollen Cloak (*Khirqa*) 15

2.1.2 Seclusion (*Khalwa*) 17

2.1.3 Remembrance of Allah's Name and Remembrance through Negation and Affirmation (*Dhikr*) 19

2.1.4 Limiting Food, Sleep and Speech 21

2.1.5 Listening to Spiritual Auditions (*Samāʿ*) 28

2.2 Principles of Sufism from the Practices of the Companions 29
2.2.1 Pledge of Allegiance (*Bayʿa*) 31
2.2.2 Keeping the Company of a Spiritual Guide (*Ṣuḥba*) 33
2.2.3 Sittings of Remembrance and Reflection (*Majālis al-Dhikr wa al-Fikr*) 37
2.2.4 Visualisation of the Spiritual Guide (*Taṣawwur al-Shaykh*) 39
2.2.5 Woollen Clothes 40
2.2.6 The Companions of the Veranda (*Aṣḥāb al-Ṣuffa*) – the First Group of Sufis 41

Chapter 3

THE FIVE FUNDAMENTAL REQUIREMENTS OF SUFISM 45

3.1 Acquiring Knowledge (*ʿIlm*) and Obedience to God (*Taqwā*) 47
3.2 Following a Spiritual Master (*Shaykh*) 52
Fundamental Guidance for the Seeker: Three Steps in the Struggle Against the Lower Self 62
3.3 Limiting Food, Sleep and Speech – the First Step 62
3.4 Abundant Remembrance of Allah (*Dhikr*) and Worship (*ʿIbāda*) – the Second Step 64
3.4.1 Visitation of Graves 64
3.4.2 The Etiquette of Performing *Dhikr* 67
3.4.3 The Remembrance of Negation and Affirmation (*Dhikr al-Nafī wa al-Ithbāt*) 67
3.4.4 The Method of Performing *Dhikr* 68
3.4.5 Four Types of *Dhikr* 70
3.4.6 Establishing Circles of *Dhikr* 75
3.5 Contemplation (*Tafakkur*) and Meditation (*Murāqaba*) – the Third Step 81

Chapter 4

THE FOUR ESSENTIAL HUMAN CHARACTERISTICS ACCORDING TO THE SUFIS 85

4.1 The First Characteristic: Purity (*Ṭahāra*) 86

4.2 The Second Characteristic: Submission and Humility (*Khushūʿ wa Khuḍūʿ*) 87

4.3 The Third Characteristic: Righteous Attributes (*Samāḥa*) 87

4.4 The Fourth Characteristic: Justice (*ʿAdāla*) 88

4.5 Attaining the Four Characteristics and the State of Benevolence (*Iḥsān*) 89

Chapter 5

THE SEVEN AFFINITIES 91

5.1 The Affinity of Purity (*Ṭahāra*) 91

5.2 The Affinity of Obedience (*Nisba al-Ṭāʿa*) 93

5.2.1 The First Branch: The Sweetness of Private Prayer (*Ḥalāwa al-Munājāt*) 94

5.2.2 The Second Branch: The Encompassing Mercy (*Shumūl al-Raḥma*) 96

5.2.3 The Third Branch: The Lights of Divine Names (*Anwār al-Asmāʾ al-Ilāhiyya*) 98

5.3 The Uwaysiyya Affinity (*al-Nisba al-Uwaysiyya*) 99

5.3.1 Different Levels of Souls in the Metaphysical Realm 101

5.4 The Affinity of Divine Gnosis (*Nisba al-Maʿrifa*) 103

5.5 The Affinity of Extreme Love (*Nisba al-ʿIshq*) 105

5.6 The Affinity of Ecstasy (*Nisba al-Wajd*) 106

5.7 The Affinity of Divine Oneness (*Nisba al-Tawḥīd*) 108

Chapter 6

THE SEVEN TYPES OF THE LOWER SELF 111

6.1 The Commanding Self (*al-Nafs al-Ammāra*) 111

6.2 The Condemning Self (*al-Nafs al-Lawwāma*) 118

6.3 The Inspiring Self (*al-Nafs al-Mulhima*) 123

6.4 The Contented Self (*al-Nafs al-Muṭma'inna*) 128

6.4.1 The Station of Sainthood (*Wilāya*) 128

6.4.2 The Opening of the Two Paths 131

6.5 The Pleasing Self (*al-Nafs al-Rāḍiya*) 138

6.6 The Pleased Self (*al-Nafs al-Marḍiyya*) 142

6.7 The Perfect Self (*al-Nafs al-Kāmila* [*al-Ṣāfiya*]) 146

6.8 The Perfect Self (*al-Nafs al-Kāmila*), the Muhammadan Station (*Maqām al-Muḥammadiyya*) and the Court of Divine Majesty (*Ḥaḍra al-Ulūhiyya*) 156

Bibliography 159

1

SUFISM IN ISLAMIC HISTORY

Sufism (*taṣawwuf*) – the spiritual and mystical dimension of Islam – is firmly rooted in the Qur'ān, Sunna and the example of the pious predecessors. The Holy Qur'ān directs the attention of its readers to a specific branch of Islam, which is a critical component of prophethood, termed as *tazkiya* (spiritual purification). Purifying the soul is amongst the four primary duties of prophethood. Allah ﷻ states:

﴿هُوَ ٱلَّذِى بَعَثَ فِى ٱلْأُمِّيِّـۧنَ رَسُولًا مِّنْهُمْ يَتْلُوا۟ عَلَيْهِمْ ءَايَـٰتِهِۦ وَيُزَكِّيهِمْ وَيُعَلِّمُهُمُ ٱلْكِتَـٰبَ وَٱلْحِكْمَةَ وَإِن كَانُوا۟ مِن قَبْلُ لَفِى ضَلَـٰلٍ مُّبِينٍ﴾

He is the One Who sent a (Glorious) Messenger (ﷺ) amongst the illiterate people from amongst themselves who recites to them His Revelations and cleanses and purifies them (outwardly and inwardly) and teaches them the Book and wisdom. Indeed, they were in open error before (his most welcome arrival).[1]

The meaning of *tazkiya* is to adorn the lower self (*nafs*) with the highest of moral values and to purify it from lowly attributes. The most splendid model of *tazkiya* is seen in the lives of the Companions. Their sincerity and their morals were an embodiment of *tazkiya*. As a result,

1 Qur'ān 62:2.

they were able to establish such an exemplary society, the likes of which history fails to replicate. They also established such a just and righteous system of governance that is unparalleled.

In the hadith, in addition to *islām* (ritual practice) and *īmān* (belief), the Holy Prophet Muhammad ﷺ mentioned *iḥsān* (spiritual excellence) as a third dimension to the religion of Islam. *Iḥsān* (spiritual excellence) denotes a state of certainty and presence for which every believer should be striving and the fondness for which should blossom in every heart. The Holy Prophet ﷺ was asked: 'What is *iḥsān* (spiritual excellence)?', and he ﷺ replied,

أَنْ تَعْبُدَ اللهَ كَأَنَّكَ تَرَاهُ، فَإِنْ لَمْ تَكُنْ تَرَاهُ فَإِنَّهُ يَرَاكَ.

> That you worship Allah ﷻ in such a state that you see Him, and if you cannot see Him then worship Him in a state acknowledging that He is seeing you.[2]

There are two aspects to the Sharia and the teachings of the Holy Prophet ﷺ: the external aspect and the internal aspect. The external aspect covers the physical acts of worship and observable practices such as the ritual standing (*qiyām*), sitting (*quʿūd*), bowing (*rukūʿ*), prostration (*sujūd*), recitation (*tilāwa*), glorification (*tasbīḥ*), supplication (*duʿā*), legal rulings (*aḥkām*) and pilgrimage rites (*manāsik*). The science of hadith preserved this through narration and compilation, and the science of *fiqh* took upon itself the task of deriving laws from them. The hadith scholars and jurists preserved and protected the *dīn* of Allah ﷻ in such a way that it can be easily practised by Muslims today.

The second aspect comprises of those internal states that run concurrently with the physical acts and practices. These internal states can be seen in the acts and practices performed by the Holy Prophet ﷺ during his life in various fields, such as worship, preaching, family

---

[2] Narrated by al-Bukhārī in *al-Ṣaḥīḥ*: *Kitāb al-Īmān* [The Book of Faith], chapter: 'Jibrīl asking the Holy Prophet ﷺ about *īmān*, *islām*, *iḥsān* and the knowledge of the Hour', 1:19 §50 & *Kitāb al-Tafsīr* [The Book of Exegesis], chapter: 'The Statement of Allah the Exalted: "*Verily, Allah! With Him (Alone) is the knowledge of the Hour*"', 6:115 §4777; and Muslim in *al-Ṣaḥīḥ*: *Kitāb al-Īmān* [The Book of Faith], chapter: 'What is *īmān*? Explaining its characteristics', 1:36 §8.

life, Jihad etc. These internal states can be defined as sincerity (*ikhlāṣ*), self-accountability (*iḥtisāb*), patience (*ṣabr*), trust in Allah (*tawakkul*), asceticism (*zuhd*), renunciation (*istighnāʾ*), altruism (*īthār*), generosity (*sakhāwa*), respect (*adab*), modesty (*hayāʾ*), sincere humility and submission of the heart (*khushūʿ* and *khuḍūʿ*), returning to Allah (*ināba*), crying and pleading before Allah (*taḍarruʿ*), feeling broken at the time of *duʿā*, preferring the hereafter to the world, seeking Allah's pleasure and the Beatific Vision and many other similar internal states and morals. The role of all these states is equivalent to that of the soul in the human body.

1.1 A Brief Historical View on Sufism in Muslim Lands

In every generation, there has always been the need for powerful personalities and propagators embodying all-encompassing qualities, who fulfilled the duties of teaching the Holy Qurʾān and the Sunna, and of internal purification (*tazkiya*). After the termination of the process of prophethood, they became the vicegerents of the Holy Prophet Muhammad ﷺ. They connected the Muslim community (*umma*) with Allah ﷻ and His Messenger ﷺ and helped them to renew the covenant that every Muslim had committed to by making the declaration of faith. They taught Muslims to take Allah ﷻ and His Messenger ﷺ as a standard in every matter of life, to be obedient and to oppose the lower self (*nafs*) and the devil (*shayṭān*). Furthermore, to reject evil (*ṭāghūt*) and to struggle for the sake of Allah Almighty, and to make this renewal of the covenant pledged to the Messenger of Allah ﷻ a way of life.

After the Rightly Guided Caliphate, the sultans neglected this aforementioned duty and focussed upon political domination and further conquests alongside extracting taxes. They also had a keen interest in securing and prolonging their dynastic rule. The religious scholars themselves needed spiritual correction so were unable to perform this duty. Besides, they were so busy in teaching, delivering sermons and writing books that they did not have the time to even think about it. Even if they had thought about fulfilling this duty, they were not up to it. The public knew them very well and were aware how very little of asceticism (*zuhd*), sincerity (*ikhlāṣ*) and the signs and qualities of the prophetic vicegerency they possessed.

Thus, religious consciousness gradually began to wane in every section of society, among the masses and the elite, to the extent that they started to forget that Islam was in reality a covenant between people and their Lord. As a result, the Islamic teachings no longer kept a check and balance upon their deeds, and the desires and lusts of their lower selves were in total control. They were like herds of sheep that have neither a shepherd nor a purpose. The desire to gain the yearning to worship, the grade of *iḥsān* and the sweetness of faith (*īmān*) became weak. Religious will and determination weakened to such an extent that people in general – except those whom Allah ﷻ had protected – chased after their lusts and desires uncontrollably.

Eventually, the Islamic Caliphate was devoid of its soul and the prophetic trust was reduced to mere governance and politics – its sole duty being collecting taxes. At that time, all across the Muslim lands, the real vicegerents of the Holy Prophet ﷺ, who were sincere men of truth, stood up and rose above the decay. Their propagation and company had such an effect upon people that they began to re-enter into the Islamic covenant. Although the people were born Muslims and had previously accepted Islam according to tradition, they were entering into this new world intentionally with complete understanding and awareness. Through their education and spiritual training, they renewed their faith and freed themselves from the dominance of the lower self (*nafs*), from being chained to their desires and from being enslaved to fellow human beings. Instead, they turned their attention to worship and obedience, calling others to Allah ﷻ and struggling in the true path.

Then, following this, from their inheritors and students, and from amongst all of those people who followed their teachings, came great flag bearers of Islamic propagation and Imams of Islamic training in the middle and later centuries. These Imams then safeguarded the soul of Islam and religious consciousness. They promoted Islamic propagation and struggling in the cause of Allah ﷻ, and they countered base desires and inclinations. If it was not for them, materialism which was engulfing civilisation, would have overtaken the entire Muslim world, and the flame of life itself would have dimmed. They were responsible for the propagation of Islam in lands far and wide where Muslim forces had not entered, such as Africa, Indonesia, the islands of the Indian Ocean, China and East India.

Then a time came in the 7th century *hijrī*, a time of depression and decay, when the Mongols turned the Islamic world upside down and left it in complete disarray. The power to fight back had completely vanished and nobody had the courage to face them. Melancholy overcame the Muslims; they sheathed their swords and became convinced that it was impossible to defeat the Tartars. They began to believe that Islam had no future, and that the Islamic world was destined to remain enslaved to this wild and barbaric nation. At this time of need, it was the same brand of righteous propagators of Islam, known as the Sufis, who mingled with these cold-hearted people and opened up their hearts to Islam. The names of most of these Sufi Imams have been airbrushed out of the history of Islamic propagation and reform. Eventually, the Tatars developed regard and love for these Imams of Sufism resulting in great numbers of them accepting Islam. Not long since the Tartar invasion, that a great number of them came into the fold of Islam and they went onto becoming the guardians of Islam with many great jurists, scholars, Sufis and military commanders coming out of their ranks.

There is no doubt that without these Sufi Imams, the Islamic civilisation would have collapsed long ago and whatever little of faith that had remained would have been destroyed by materialism. The relationship of the heart with Allah ﷻ, life with spirituality and society with morality would have been disconnected. Sincerity would cease to exist, and spiritual illnesses would have multiplied. The diseases of the heart would have spread without there being a physician to cure them. People would be lost in materialism and religious scholars would be pursuing wealth and status and would be competing with one other. They would have been overtaken by jealousy and greed. Thus, the branch of Islam that is an integral part of the duties of prophethood (i.e. internal purification) would have been totally lost.

Then again in the last two centuries, since the Muslim *Umma*'s political, economic, cultural, social, academic and moral affairs were dislodged and destroyed by colonial conspiracies and by the bad character and lavish lifestyles of the elites, a disturbing vacuum has been left in this regard. In reality, this vacuum is so vast that its effects have penetrated deeply into individual life as well as in society. It is imperative to fill this vacuum so that the true Sufism (*taṣawwuf*), *tazkiya* and *iḥsān* are revived once again, as it was by the pious predecessors in their respective periods. This should be carried out following the methodology adopted by the Holy Prophet ﷺ and the teachings of the Qur'ān and *Sunna*. It should be carried out in every period and wherever Muslims are settled.

The comprehensive system of the purification of the lower self (*nafs*) and the rectification of morals in later centuries developed into a fully-fledged science and discipline known as '*taṣawwuf*' (Sufism). Its practitioner would be labelled as '*ṣūfī*'. The remit of this science was: to pinpoint the deception and deceit of the lower self (*nafs*) and of the devil; to rectify moral degeneracy, to control carnal desires and to cure the diseases of the heart; and to explain in detail the method of attaining connection with Allah ﷻ and to attain His pleasure and nearness. The foundations of this science were grounded in the concepts of '*tazkiya*' (spiritual purification) and '*iḥsān*' (spiritual and moral excellence) as expounded in the Qur'ān and hadith. The term '*taṣawwuf*' (Sufism) is the technical designation for the study of '*tazkiya*' (spiritual purification) and '*iḥsān*' (spiritual and moral excellence) when it later developed into a formal discipline and science.

The great authorities of Islam throughout the ages declared the science of '*taṣawwuf*' (Sufism) to be an invaluable and indispensable service to Islam, and they deemed it the greater *jihad* as it was a means of reinvigorating spiritual life to the heart and soul of the *Umma* and curing its malaise and spiritual diseases. Due to the efforts of the Sufis and those who were trained by them, Islam was propagated far and wide to distant lands where even the Muslim armies had not reached, such as Bangladesh, Malaysia, Indonesia and West Africa. In these lands, millions were brought into the fold of Islam. It was the result of the teachings and endeavours of the great Sufis, who filled the Muslim societies with faith, certainty and virtue, that led to the masses becoming Muslims. The Sufis also played an important role in many of the military expeditions and significant conquests throughout the centuries. Thus, to reject the role played by the Sufis and their services and contributions to the cause of Islam would be a grave injustice and prejudice to Islamic history.

In the science of hadith, a *'mutawātir'* hadith is a narration that a large number of narrators have transmitted in every generation with an unbroken chain that anyone with sound intellect would find it impossible to accept that all of the narrators colluded to fabricate it. The hadith-scholars have declared such narrations to being unanimously accepted. If we adopt the same logic of the hadith-scholars, we can categorically say that even a cursory study of history makes it clear that from the early generations till today, in every period without any exception, a great number of unanimously accepted scholars, such as the four Imams, adopted the Sufi path. They enriched their own lives through the teachings of *taṣawwuf* and benefitted others by propagating it. They dedicated their lives in its propagation and were certain about its authenticity and effectiveness. They were the jewels of their respective eras and societies. They were not only superior to their contemporaries in righteousness, sincerity and inner piety but also the scholarly exemplars in their knowledge of the Qur'ān, their love for the Sunna and their aversion to religious innovations.

It is possible for one, two or ten people to wrongly gather upon something or be the target of a conspiracy but for hundreds of thousands of people who are amongst the foremost in knowledge and practice to have been in error for centuries is beyond comprehension. Furthermore, millions of people being guided by these Sufi scholars and then excelling in inner perfection is a proof that is proven by history and cannot be disputed. It is also illogical and totally against common sense that this great number of Sufi scholars who were in different time periods and geographical locations could all continually and persistently remain upon the path of *taṣawwuf* in error. If they were in error Allah ﷻ would have guided them as He states in the Holy Qur'ān:

﴿وَٱلَّذِينَ جَٰهَدُواْ فِينَا لَنَهۡدِيَنَّهُمۡ سُبُلَنَاۚ وَإِنَّ ٱللَّهَ لَمَعَ
ٱلۡمُحۡسِنِينَ﴾

> *And those who strive hard (and struggle against the lower self vehemently) for Our cause, We certainly guide them to Our ways, and verily Allah blesses the men of spiritual excellence with His companionship.*[3]

If any of these great Sufi scholars, who were the pillars of light of their respective eras, were to be erased from history then there would be nothing left to show for Islamic scholarship and the propagation of Islam. If they cannot be trusted, then there is no other category of people in Islamic history that are worthy of trust.[4]

1.2 The Two Dimensions of Islam and the Two Promises for its Preservation

We will paraphrase the opening chapter of Shāh Walī Allāh's book '*Hamaʿāt*'. In this very beneficial discourse, he states: Allah ﷻ sent the Holy Prophet ﷺ for the guidance of mankind. For the purpose of the establishment and preservation of Islam, He ﷻ promised to help the Holy Prophet ﷺ with two promises. The first of the two promise is:

﴿لِيُظۡهِرَهُۥ عَلَى ٱلدِّينِ كُلِّهِۦ﴾

> *To make him (the Messenger) dominant over every (other exponent of) Din (Religion).*[5]

And the second promise is:

﴿وَإِنَّا لَهُۥ لَحَٰفِظُونَ﴾

> *And surely, We alone will guard it.*[6]

These two promises are regarding the establishment and preservation of Islam. Thus, through this divine help, Allah ﷻ made Islam

---

[3] Qur'ān 29:69.

[4] Abū al-Ḥasan ʿAlī al-Nadwī, *Tazkiya-o-Iḥsān yā Taṣawwuf-o-Sulūk*.

[5] Qur'ān 9:33.

[6] Qur'ān 15:9.

dominant over all other religions. The objective of propagating Islam was to guide Arabs and non-Arabs and to totally eradicate injustice, oppression and disorder.

In order to fulfil the first promise, the state of Madina was established. Then a long struggle led to the conquest of Makkah and of the entire Arabian Peninsula during the time of the Holy Prophet ﷺ. Later the Eastern Roman Empire, Syria and Persia were also conquered during the time of the Rightly Guided Caliphate and those who followed them. After this, Islam's power and rule continued to grow. This establishment of Islam was completed by the Rightly Guided Caliphs and the later rulers.

Regarding the second promise of the protection of Islam, it is necessary to know that Islam has two dimensions: the outer and the inner. The purpose of the outer dimension is the protection of the public interest and welfare. In order to realise this, those rulings that deal with this need to be implemented and also propagated. Anything that has a negative impact upon the public interest and welfare should be strictly prohibited. The purpose of the inner dimension is to acquire those states that are present in the heart after the performance of virtuous deeds. When it is clear that Islam has an outer dimension and an inner dimension then it must also be accepted that with regards to the protection of Islam, it will also have two dimensions.

After the passing of the Holy Prophet ﷺ, there were two ways by which the promise to provide protection was fulfilled. One was that those who had the capacity to protect the Shariah, took on the protection of the outer dimension. They comprised the jurists, hadith scholars, soldiers and reciters, amongst others. Such people are seen to be active in every period. Whenever there was an attempt to alter or distort Islam in any way, they stood up against it. They motivated Muslims to study Islamic sciences. Among them, every hundred years a revivalist (*mujaddid*) is born who has the duty of reviving the religion. Generally, these revivalists revive the outward dimension, but every so often, after a very long period, a *mujaddid* comes who is given the duty of reviving both the inward and outward.

The second group of people are those who Allah ﷻ has granted the ability to protect the inner dimension of Islam, which is known as *taṣawwuf* and *iḥsān*. In every period, the public has turned to the Sufi saints and scholars. They invite people to be pious and virtuous so that they experience the positive effects against the lower self (*nafs*) and spiritual delight in the heart through the performance of righteous deeds. Furthermore, they teach people to adopt virtuous morals. In every period there are some Sufi scholars who are known as the Saints (*Awliyāʾ Allāh*), and they have been given the God-given ability to establish the inner dimension of the religion and to propagate it to people.

The inner dimension of the religion is in fact the essence of Islam – the reality of which is known as '*iḥsān*'. *Iḥsān* is to worship Allah ﷻ as though one sees Him ﷻ, and if that is not possible, then one should know that Allah ﷻ sees them. Allah ﷻ makes these Sufi scholars the manifestation of *iḥsān* among the people. They work for the propagation and protection of the inner dimension of the religion.

One of the signs of the Saints (*Awliyāʾ Allāh*), who in particular become the manifestation of *iḥsān*, is that people recognise their lofty spiritual status and are attracted towards them. Those invocations (*adhkār*) and litanies (*waẓāʾif*) that already existed among the *Umma* which people are naturally inclined towards are infused into the hearts of these Saints (*Awliyāʾ Allāh*). Their words and company (*suḥba*) have the extraordinary power of enabling people to accept and act upon their teachings. They perform all types of miracles (*karamāt*). Through divine disclosure (*kashf*) and miracles (*karamāt*), they know the spiritual state of people's hearts. Through the help and assistance from Allah ﷻ, they have the power to take control of some worldly matters. Their supplications are accepted in the court of Allah ﷻ. This, along with many other miracles of this kind, take place due to their constant struggle. As a result of this, they have a great number of disciples, seekers and followers. To carry out inner reformation of the masses they reformulate routines for daily litanies and spiritual practices. In this way, the foundations of a new branch of a spiritual order (*ṭarīqa*) are laid down which people start to follow. The increase in blessings (*baraka*) and effectiveness of these spiritual orders is such that disciples and seekers quickly reach their desired goal.

Just like the revival and reformation of the outer dimension of the religion, the revival and reformation of the inner dimension of the religion also continues simultaneously in every period. Just as schools of thought come into existence for the outer dimension of Islam, in the same way spiritual orders come into existence for the inner dimension of Islam. The differences in the teachings, routines for litanies, invocations and spiritual practices among the different spiritual orders is similar to the jurisprudential differences between the schools of thought. Practically, it is similar to the different treatments prescribed by different doctors. The reason for having different spiritual orders is that people have different spiritual temperaments and dispositions. However, the purpose of all of them is the same.

2

PRINCIPLES OF SUFISM IN THE ERA OF THE HOLY PROPHET ﷺ AND THE COMPANIONS

Along with providing people with the blessing of Islam, the Holy Prophet ﷺ also provided them a way of life by providing a framework for an Islamic society. In the history of Islam, those periods that are considered to be exemplary are that of the Holy Prophet ﷺ, the Companions and the Successors. Many hadiths are testimony to this, for instance:

قَالَ: خَيْرُ النَّاسِ قَرْنِي ثُمَّ الَّذِينَ يَلُونَهُمْ ثُمَّ الَّذِينَ يَلُونَهُمْ.

> The Holy Prophet ﷺ said, "The best people are from my generation, then those who follow them, then those who follow them."[7]

قَالَ: خَيْرُ أُمَّتِي الْقَرْنُ الَّذِينَ يَلُونِي، ثُمَّ الَّذِينَ يَلُونَهُمْ ثُمَّ الَّذِينَ يَلُونَهُمْ.

---

[7] Narrated by al-Bukhārī in *al-Ṣaḥīḥ*: *Kitāb al-Shahādāt* [The Book of Testimonies], chapter: 'Do not be a witness for injustice, if asked for that', 2:938 §2509.

He ﷺ said, "The best of my community is the period that is connected to me, then those who are connected to them, then those who are connected to them."[8]

2.1 Principles of Sufism from the Sunna

The life of the Holy Prophet Muhammad ﷺ can be divided into two parts: the one before the declaration of Prophethood and the one after. Both are a model of perfection for humanity. The following verses from the Holy Qur'ān are evidence of this:

﴿فَقَدْ لَبِثْتُ فِيكُمْ عُمُرًا مِّن قَبْلِهِۦٓ أَفَلَا تَعْقِلُونَ﴾

I have indeed spent a (part of) life amongst you (even) before this (revelation of the Qur'ān). So do you not understand?[9]

﴿لَّقَدْ كَانَ لَكُمْ فِى رَسُولِ ٱللَّهِ أُسْوَةٌ حَسَنَةٌ لِّمَن كَانَ يَرْجُوا ٱللَّهَ وَٱلْيَوْمَ ٱلْءَاخِرَ وَذَكَرَ ٱللَّهَ كَثِيرًا﴾

In truth, in (the sacred person of) Allah's Messenger (ﷺ) there is for you a most perfect and beautiful model (of life).[10]

It must be kept in mind that everything is carried out for a specific purpose. For instance, food is eaten to remove hunger but if there is no hunger then there is no need of food. Medicine is taken to cure an illness but if there is no illness then there is no need to take medicine. In the same way, the purpose of spiritual training and struggle on the Sufi path is to purify the lower self (*nafs*) and the inner self. If one is already pure from moral and spiritual ailments and is upon the highest level of internal purification, then there is no need to become a seeker upon the path of Sufism (*taṣawwuf*).

---

[8] Narrated by Muslim in *al-Ṣaḥīḥ*: *Kitāb Faḍā'il al-Saḥāba* [The Book of Virtues of the Companions], chapter: 'The excellence of the Companions, then those who follow them, and then those who follow them', 4:1962 §2533.

[9] Qur'ān 10:16.

[10] Qur'ān 33:21.

The starting point of the Holy Prophet's spiritual state is higher than the highest grades obtained through Sainthood (*wilāya*). This is why he ﷺ did not need to practise Sufism (*taṣawwuf*) and adopt the Sufi path. However, as the Holy Prophet ﷺ is the greatest exemplar of virtue, his practice and mannerism became the principles of Sufism (*taṣawwuf*) that were later adopted by the Sufis. Below, some Sufi practices will be discussed in light of the Sunna.

2.1.1 WEARING THE WOOLLEN CLOAK (KHIRQA)

To wear a woollen cloak (*khirqa*) is not an essential requirement of Sufism (*taṣawwuf*), however, the Sufis of the first and the middle periods preferred it, as it embodied humility and simplicity. They wore woollen cloaks for spiritual training (*mujāhada*). Wearing a woollen cloak is one of the reasons behind referring to the practitioners of *taṣawwuf* as 'Ṣūfī', as it is derived from the word 'ṣūf' (wool).

The Holy Prophet ﷺ used to love wearing woollen garments. The practice of the Sufis in wearing woollen cloaks is thus derived from the Sunna. Mughīra b. Shuʿba ؓ narrates:

فَغَسَلَ وَجْهَهُ وَيَدَيْهِ وَعَلَيْهِ جُبَّةٌ مِنْ صُوفٍ.

> The Holy Prophet ﷺ washed his face and his hands, and at that time he was wearing a robe made from wool.[11]

Anas b. Mālik ؓ narrates:

لَبِسَ رَسُولُ اللهِ ﷺ الصُّوفَ.

> The Messenger of Allah ﷺ wore woollen clothes.[12]

In another narration, it is stated:

كَانَ رَسُولُ اللهِ ﷺ يَلْبَسُ الصُّوفَ.

---

[11] Narrated by al-Bukhārī in *al-Ṣaḥīḥ*: *Kitāb al-Libās* [The Book of Clothing], chapter: 'Wearing a woollen cloak during a battle', 5:2185 §5463.

[12] Narrated by Ibn Mājah in *al-Sunan*: *Kitāb al-Aṭʿima* [The Book of Foods], chapter: 'The bread of wheat', 2:1111 §3348.

The Messenger of Allah ﷺ used to wear clothing made from wool.[13]

Sayyida ʿĀʾisha al-Ṣiddīqa ؓ states:

$$\text{صَنَعْتُ لَهُ ثَوْبًا مِنْ صُوفٍ فَلَبِسَهُ.}$$

I made a garment of wool for the Holy Prophet ﷺ and he wore it.[14]

Abū Burda ؓ relates:

$$\text{دَخَلْتُ عَلَى عَائِشَةَ ؓ فَأَخْرَجَتْ إِلَيْنَا إِزَارًا غَلِيظًا مِمَّا يُصْنَعُ بِالْيَمَنِ وَكِسَاءً مِنَ الَّتِي يُسَمُّونَهَا الْمُلَبَّدَةَ - قَالَ - فَأَقْسَمَتْ بِاللهِ إِنَّ رَسُولَ اللهِ ﷺ قُبِضَ فِي هَذَيْنِ الثَّوْبَيْنِ.}$$

I visited ʿĀʾisha ؓ and she brought out for us the coarse lower garment made in Yemen and a cloak made from something known as 'al-Mulabbada' (i.e. wool felt). She swore by Allah ﷻ that Allah's Messenger ﷺ died in these two clothes.[15]

In this narration, the word 'kisāʾ' (cloak) has been used. According to the hadith scholars, the meaning of this word is 'ridāʾ min al-ṣūf' (an outer garment made of wool).[16]

In ʿUmda al-Qārī, Imam Badr al-Dīn al-ʿAynī writes:

---

[13] Al-Qasṭallānī, al-Mawāhib al-Ladunniyya bi al-Minaḥ al-Muḥammadiyya, 2:192.

[14] Al-Fayrūzābādī, Safr al-Saʿāda, p.218.

[15] Narrated by al-Bukhārī in al-Ṣaḥīḥ: Kitāb Abwāb al-Khumus [The Book of the One-Fifth Tax], chapter: 'What is mentioned concerning the Prophet's coat of mail...', 3:1133 §2941; Muslim in al-Ṣaḥīḥ: Kitāb al-Libās wa al-Zīna [The Book of Clothing and Adornment], chapter: 'Humility in dress and sticking to coarse and simple clothes, 3:1649 §2080; and al-Tirmidhī in al-Sunan: Kitāb al-Libās [The Book of Clothing], chapter: 'What is mentioned concerning wearing wool', 4:224 §1733; and Ibn Ḥibbān in al-Ṣaḥīḥ, 4:593 §6623-6624.

[16] Al-Qasṭallānī, Irshād al-Sārī Sharḥ Ṣaḥīḥ al-Bukhārī, 5:200.

اَلْكِسَاءُ مَعْرُوفٌ وَلَكِنَّ الظَّاهِرَ أَنَّهُ لَا يُطْلَقُ إِلَّا عَلَى مَا كَانَ مِنَ الصُّوفِ.

> '*Kisā*'' (cloak) is well-known, however, its apparent meaning is not applied except to what is made from wool.[17]

It is clear from this report that at the time of his passing, the Holy Prophet ﷺ was wearing a garment made from wool. It is for this reason that the Sufis adorned themselves with woollen garments and made it their symbol. Such reports corroborate the narrations transmitted related in the books of *taṣawwuf* by eminent Sufis such as Imam al-Qushayrī and Imam Abū Naṣr al-Sirāj al-Ṭūsī.

2.1.2 SECLUSION (KHALWA)

From his childhood, the Holy Prophet ﷺ was inclined towards remaining in solitude. Al-Ḥalabī mentions the Holy Prophet's ﷺ tendency towards seclusion. He says:

أَلَّفَ الْعِبَادَةَ وَالْخَلْوَةَ فِي حَالِ كَوْنِهِ طِفْلًا.

> He developed great affection for worship and seclusion while he was still a child.[18]

However, when the declaration of Prophethood came near, there was a great increase in the desire to remain in seclusion. Sayyida 'Ā'isha ﵂ states:

ثُمَّ حُبِّبَ إِلَيْهِ الْخَلَاءُ وَكَانَ يَخْلُو بِغَارِ حِرَاءٍ فَيَتَحَنَّثُ فِيهِ وَهُوَ التَّعَبُّدُ اللَّيَالِي ذَوَاتَ الْعَدَدِ.

> Then remaining in solitude became beloved to him, so he used to remain in seclusion in the Cave of Ḥirā' where he used to worship for many nights.[19]

---

[17] Badr al-Dīn al-'Aynī, *'Umda al-Qārī*, 15:32.

[18] Al-Ḥalabī, *al-Sīra al-Ḥalabiyya*, 1:382.

[19] Narrated by al-Bukhārī in *al-Ṣaḥīḥ*: *Kitāb Bad' al-Waḥy* [The Book on the

She also stated:

وَحَبَّبَ اللهُ تَعَالَى إِلَيْهِ الْخَلْوَةَ، فَلَمْ يَكُنْ شَيْءٌ أَحَبَّ إِلَيْهِ مِنْ أَنْ يَخْلُوَ وَحْدَهُ.

> Allah ﷻ made being in seclusion beloved to him and there was nothing more beloved to him than remaining in seclusion.[20]

Mullā ʿAlī al-Qārī states that this period of seclusion by the Holy Prophet ﷺ lasted for three to seven days or at times for thirty to forty days. The practice of the Sufis to go into seclusion for forty days is derived from this practice of the Holy Prophet ﷺ.[21]

During this seclusion, the Holy Prophet ﷺ worshipped according to the Sharia of Prophet Ibrāhīm ﷺ which consisted of the remembrance of Allah ﷻ, contemplation and meditation.[22]

Seclusion (*khalwa*) is an important practice among the Sufis. On the importance of seclusion and relating their experiences of it, the following are some statements given by them.

According to Yaḥyā b. Muʿādh:

مَنْ كَانَ أُنْسُهُ بِالْخَلْوَةِ ذَهَبَ أُنْسُهُ إِذَا فَارَقَهَا، وَمَنْ كَانَ أُنْسُهُ بِاللهِ فِي الْخَلْوَةِ اسْتَوَتْ عِنْدَهُ الْأَمَاكِنُ كُلُّهَا.

> Whoever's comfort is in seclusion, his comfort will go when he leaves the seclusion. And whoever's comfort is in Allah ﷻ whilst in seclusion, for him all places are equal.[23]

According to Abū Bakr al-Warrāq:

Commencement of Revelation], chapter: 'How was the beginning of revelation to Allah's Messenger ﷺ', 1:4 §3.

[20] Ibn Hishām, *Sīra Ibn Hishām*, 1:234.

[21] Mullā ʿAlī al-Qārī, *Mirqāt al-Mafātīḥ*, 5:401.

[22] Al-Fayrūzābādī, *Safr al-Saʿāda*, p.26.

[23] Ibn Abī Bakr al-Rāzī, *Ḥadāʾiq al-Ḥaqāʾiq*, p.41.

وَجَدْتُ خَيْرَ الدُّنْيَا وَالْآخِرَةِ فِي الْعُزْلَةِ وَالْخَلْوَةِ، وَشَرَّهُمَا فِي الْخُلْطَةِ.

I have found the goodness of this life and the hereafter in solitude and seclusion, and their evil in mingling (with others).[24]

According to Abū Bakr al-Shiblī:

عَلَامَةُ الْإِفْلَاسِ الْاِسْتِئْنَاسُ بِالنَّاسِ.

The sign of bankruptcy is wanting to socialise with people.[25]

And it is said:

إِذَا أَرَادَ اللهُ أَنْ يَنْقُلَ الْعَبْدَ مِنْ ذُلِّ الْمَعْصِيَةِ إِلَى عِزِّ الطَّاعَةِ آنَسَهُ بِالْوَحْدَةِ، وَأَغْنَاهُ بِالْقَنَاعَةِ، وَبَصَّرَهُ عُيُوبَ نَفْسِهِ، فَمَنْ أُعْطِيَ ذَلِكَ، فَقَدْ أُعْطِيَ خَيْرَ الدُّنْيَا وَالْآخِرَةِ.

When Allah ﷻ wants to take a servant from the infamy of disobedience to the honour of obedience, He makes him find delight in solitude, and gives him self-sufficiency through contentment, and makes him see his own faults. And whosoever is given that, he has indeed been given the best of this world and the life hereafter.[26]

2.1.3 Remembrance of Allah's Name and Remembrance through Negation and Affirmation (Dhikr)

The Holy Prophet ﷺ was instructed in the Holy Qur'ān to perform the remembrance (*dhikr*) of the personal name of the Necessary Being, Allah ﷻ. Allah ﷻ says:

---

24 Ibid., p.42.

25 Ibid.

26 Ibid.

﴿وَٱذۡكُرِ ٱسۡمَ رَبِّكَ وَتَبَتَّلۡ إِلَيۡهِ تَبۡتِيلٗا﴾

And continue remembering the Name of your Lord, devoted completely to Him alone (in your heart and soul), broken away from everyone else.[27]

Al-Qāḍī Thanā' Allāh Pānī Pattī states:

اِعْلَمْ أَنَّ عَلَى هَذَا التَّأْوِيلِ فِي قَوْلِهِ تَعَالَى وَاذْكُرِ اسْمَ رَبِّكَ إِشَارَةً إِلَى تَكْرِيرِ اسْمِ الذَّاتِ.

Let it be known that in the saying of Allah, '*Remember the name of your Lord,*' is an indication towards repeating the personal name of Allah.[28]

The Holy Prophet ﷺ was instructed in the Qur'ān to perform the remembrance of Allah ﷻ through the 'remembrance of negation and affirmation' (*dhikr al-nafī wa al-ithbāt*), i.e. *Lā ilāha illā Allāh* (there is no God but Allah). Allah ﷻ states:

﴿رَّبُّ ٱلۡمَشۡرِقِ وَٱلۡمَغۡرِبِ لَآ إِلَٰهَ إِلَّا هُوَ﴾

He is the Lord of the east and the west. There is no God but He.[29]

In his exegesis of this verse, Qāḍī Thanā' Allāh Pānī Pattī states:

وَفِي قَوْلِهِ تَعَالَى: ﴿رَّبُّ ٱلۡمَشۡرِقِ وَٱلۡمَغۡرِبِ لَآ إِلَٰهَ إِلَّا هُوَ﴾ عَلَى قِرَاءَةِ الْجَرِّ إِشَارَةٌ إِلَى تَصَوُّرِ إِحَاطَتِهِ تَعَالَى بِالْمُمْكِنَاتِ ذِكْرُ النَّفْيِ وَالْإِثْبَاتِ وَكُلَّا التَّكْرِيرَيْنِ أَسَاسَانِ بِطَرِيقَةِ أَرْبَابِ كَمَالَاتِ الْوِلَايَاتِ.

---

27 Qur'ān 73:8.

28 Qāḍī Thanā' Allāh Pānī Pattī, *Tafsīr al-Maẓharī*, 10:111.

29 Qur'ān 73:8.

> In the saying of Allah ﷻ, *'He is the Lord of the east and the west. There is no God but He,'* there is an indication to the concept of Allah's encompassment of all possible existents (i.e creation) in the remembrance of negation and affirmation (*dhikr al-nafī wa al-ithbāt*). Both of these statements are the basis of the path of the perfect saints.[30]

Furthermore, the Holy Prophet ﷺ declared the 'remembrance of negation and affirmation' (*dhikr al-nafī wa al-ithbāt*) to be the best invocation (*dhikr*). He mentioned its numerous merits and instructed the Muslims to perform the remembrance of Allah (*dhikr*) by reciting it. This remembrance is a mainstay of the spiritual path adopted by the Sufi shaykhs and instructed by them to their disciples.

2.1.4 LIMITING FOOD, SLEEP AND SPEECH

On the importance of eating, sleeping and speaking less, Bakr b. ʿAbd Allāh al-Muzanī states:

ثَلَاثَةٌ يُحِبُّهُمُ اللهُ تَعَالَى: رَجُلٌ قَلِيلُ الْأَكْلِ، قَلِيلُ النَّوْمِ، قَلِيلُ الرَّاحَةِ. وَثَلَاثَةٌ يُبْغِضُهُمُ اللهُ تَعَالَى: رَجُلٌ كَثِيرُ الْأَكْلِ، كَثِيرُ النَّوْمِ، كَثِيرُ الرَّاحَةِ.

> Three types of people Allah ﷻ loves: a man who eats less, who sleeps less and who takes less comfort. Three types of people Allah ﷻ hates: a man who eats a lot, who sleeps a lot and who has a lot of comfort.[31]

Concerning the practice of the Holy Prophet ﷺ with respect to eating less, Sayyida ʿĀʾisha al-Ṣiddīqa رضي الله عنها states:

كَانَ يَأْتِي عَلَى آلِ مُحَمَّدٍ الشَّهْرُ مَا يُرَى فِي بَيْتٍ مِنْ بُيُوتِهِ الدُّخَانُ.

> A period of a whole month would pass over the family of the

---

30 Qāḍī Thanāʾ Allāh Pānī Pattī, *Tafsīr al-Maẓharī*, 10:111.

31 Abū Saʿd al-Nīsābūrī in *Tahdhīb al-Asrār*, p.170.

Holy Prophet Muhammad ﷺ that smoke would not be visible in any of their homes.[32]

In another narration, Sayyida ʿĀʾisha ؓ states:

مَا شَبِعَ رَسُولُ اللهِ ﷺ مِنْ خُبْزِ شَعِيرٍ يَوْمَيْنِ مُتَتَابِعَيْنِ حَتَّى قُبِضَ.

The Messenger of Allah ﷺ did not eat barley bread to his fill for two consecutive days until his passing.[33]

Abū Hurayra ؓ relates:

وَالَّذِي نَفْسِي بِيَدِهِ مَا أَشْبَعَ النَّبِيُّ ﷺ أَهْلَهُ ثَلَاثَةَ أَيَّامٍ تِبَاعًا مِنْ خُبْزِ الْحِنْطَةِ حَتَّى فَارَقَ الدُّنْيَا.

By Him in Whose Hand is my life, Allah's Messenger ﷺ did not feed his family to their full with the bread of wheat for three days successively until he left the world.[34]

Imam al-Fayrūzābādī relates:

كَانَ رَسُولُ اللهِ ﷺ يَصُومُ نَافِلَةً حَتَّى يَظُنُّوا أَنَّهُ لَا يُفْطِرُ.

The Messenger of Allah ﷺ used to fast supererogatory (*nafl*) fasts so regularly that the Companions thought he would not miss out a single day's fast.[35]

Abū Juḥayfa ؓ relates:

---

[32] Narrated by Ibn Mājah in *al-Sunan*: *Kitāb al-Zuhd* [The Book of Abstinence], chapter: 'The livelihood of the family of the Holy Prophet Muhammad ﷺ', 2:1388 §4145.

[33] Narrated by al-Tirmidhī in *al-Sunan*: *Kitāb al-Zuhd* [The Book of Abstinence], chapter: 'What has been related concerning the livelihood of the Holy Prophet Muhammad ﷺ and his family', 4:579 §2357.

[34] Narrated by Abū Saʿd al-Nīsābūrī in *Tahdhīb al-Asrār*, p.169.

[35] Al-Fayrūzābādī, *Safr al-Saʿāda*, pg.113.

أَكَلْتُ خُبْزًا وَلَحْمًا ثُمَّ أَتَيْتُ النَّبِيَّ ﷺ فَتَجَشَّأْتُ، فَقَالَ النَّبِيُّ ﷺ: أَقْصِرْ عَنَّا مِنْ جُشَائِكَ هَذَا، فَإِنَّ أَطْوَلَ النَّاسِ شَبْعًا فِي الدُّنْيَا، أَطْوَلُهُمْ جُوعًا يَوْمَ الْقِيَامَةِ.

I ate bread with meat, and then came to the Holy Prophet ﷺ, and then burped (in his blessed presence). The Holy Prophet ﷺ said: "Spare us from this burping of yours. For the most sated of people in this life are the hungriest on the Day of Judgement."[36]

With respect to the Holy Prophet's practice in sleeping less, Allah ﷻ commands in the Holy Qur'ān:

﴿يَٰٓأَيُّهَا ٱلْمُزَّمِّلُ ۝١ قُمِ ٱلَّيْلَ إِلَّا قَلِيلًا ۝٢ نِّصْفَهُۥٓ أَوِ ٱنقُصْ مِنْهُ قَلِيلًا ۝٣ أَوْ زِدْ عَلَيْهِ وَرَتِّلِ ٱلْقُرْءَانَ تَرْتِيلًا﴾

O mantled (Beloved!) Rise and stand (in Prayer) at night but (for) a short while, half the night or decrease it a little or increase a little more to it. And recite the Qur'an with most pleasant pauses.[37]

Later in the same chapter, Allah ﷻ states:

﴿إِنَّ رَبَّكَ يَعْلَمُ أَنَّكَ تَقُومُ أَدْنَىٰ مِن ثُلُثَيِ ٱلَّيْلِ وَنِصْفَهُۥ وَثُلُثَهُۥ وَطَآئِفَةٌ مِّنَ ٱلَّذِينَ مَعَكَ﴾

Surely, your Lord knows that you stand (for prayer sometimes) about two-thirds of the night and (some-times) half the night and (sometimes) a third of the night, and (also) a party of those who are with you (join in standing up for Prayer).[38]

Imam al-Baghawī states:

---

[36] Narrated by al-Bayhaqī in *Shuʿab al-Īmān*, 5:26 §5642; and al-Ḥākim in *al-Mustadrak*, 4:346 §7864.

[37] Qur'ān 73:1-4.

[38] Qur'ān 73:20.

كَانَ يُصَلِّي اللَّيْلَ كُلَّهُ فَأُمِرَهُ أَن يُّخَفِّفَ عَلَى نَفْسِهِ.

The Messenger of Allah ﷺ used to pray through the entire night, then Allah ﷻ commanded him to make it easy for himself.[39]

In another narration, he states:

كَانَ رَسُولُ اللهِ ﷺ يَجْتَهِدُ فِي الْعِبَادَةِ حَتَّى كَانَ يُرَاوِحُ بَيْنَ قَدَمَيْهِ فِي الصَّلَاةِ لِطُولِ قِيَامِهِ.

The Messenger of Allah ﷺ used to strive so much in the worship of Allah ﷻ that he used to put his weight on one leg, then on the other (to rest each leg), because of the length of his standing in prayer.[40]

Al-Mughīra b. Shuʿba ؓ relates:

أَنَّ النَّبِيَّ ﷺ صَلَّى حَتَّى انْتَفَخَتْ قَدَمَاهُ، فَقِيلَ لَهُ: أَتَكَلَّفُ هَذَا، وَقَدْ غَفَرَ اللهُ لَكَ مَا تَقَدَّمَ مِنْ ذَنْبِكَ وَمَا تَأَخَّرَ، فَقَالَ: أَفَلَا أَكُونُ عَبْدًا شَكُورًا.

The Holy Prophet ﷺ used to offer the ritual prayer till both his feet swelled. He was asked why he offered such an unbearable prayer when Allah ﷻ had forgiven him for his past and future. And the Holy Prophet ﷺ replied, "Should I not be a thankful servant."[41]

---

[39] Al-Baghawī, *Maʿālim al-Tanzīl*, 3:211.

[40] Ibid.

[41] Narrated by al-Bukhārī in *al-Ṣaḥīḥ*: *Kitāb Tafsīr al-Qurʾān* [The Book of Qurʾānic Exegesis], chapter: 'So that Allah ﷻ forgives, for your sake, all the earlier and later sins [of your *Umma*]', 4:1830 §4556 & *Kitāb al-Riqāq* [The Book of Softening the Heart], chapter: 'Patience with the prohibitions of Allah', 5:2375 §6106; and Muslim in *al-Ṣaḥīḥ*: *Kitāb Ṣifa al-Qiyāma wa al-Janna wa al-Nār* [The Book of the Description of the Day of Judgement, Paradise and the Hellfire], chapter: 'Excess in good deeds and striving in worship', 4:2171 §2819.

Al-Qāḍī ʿIyāḍ relates that Sayyida ʿĀʾisha ؓ said:

قَامَ رَسُولُ اللهِ ﷺ بِآيَةٍ مِنَ الْقُرْآنِ لَيْلَةً.

The Messenger of Allah ﷺ used to (on occasions) spend the whole night standing in prayer, contemplating upon a single verse of the Holy Qurʾān.[42]

Al-Aswad ؓ relates:

سَأَلْتُ عَائِشَةَ ؓ كَيْفَ كَانَتْ صَلَاةُ النَّبِيِّ ﷺ بِاللَّيْلِ؟ قَالَتْ: كَانَ يَنَامُ أَوَّلَهُ وَيَقُومُ آخِرَهُ، فَيُصَلِّي، ثُمَّ يَرْجِعُ إِلَى فِرَاشِهِ، فَإِذَا أَذَّنَ الْمُؤَذِّنُ وَثَبَ، فَإِنْ كَانَ بِهِ حَاجَةٌ اغْتَسَلَ، وَإِلَّا تَوَضَّأَ وَخَرَجَ.

I asked ʿĀʾisha ؓ: "How is the night prayer of the Holy Prophet ﷺ?" She replied, "He used to sleep early at night, and get up in its last part to pray, and then return to his bed. When the Muʾadhdhin would give the ādhān, he would get up. If he was in need of a bath, he would take it; otherwise, he would perform ablution and then go out (for the prayer)."[43]

On the importance of the night vigil, Fuḍayl b. ʿIyāḍ said:

مِنْ أَخْلَاقِ الْأَنْبِيَاءِ: اَلْحِلْمُ، وَالْأَنَاةُ، وَقِيَامُ اللَّيْلِ.

From the character of the Prophets are forbearance, deliberation and standing in prayer at night.[44]

---

[42] Al-Qāḍī ʿIyāḍ, al-Shifāʾ, 1:288.

[43] Narrated by al-Bukhārī in al-Ṣaḥīḥ: Kitāb al-Jumuʿa [The Book of the Friday Prayer], chapter: 'The one who sleeps the first part of the night and stays awake in the latter part', 1:385 §1095; Muslim in al-Ṣaḥīḥ: Kitāb Ṣalāt al-Musāfirīn wa Qaṣruhā [The Book of the Traveller's Prayer and its Shortening], chapter: 'The night vigil and the number of units offered by the Holy Prophet ﷺ in the night', 1:510 §739; and Aḥmad b. Ḥanbal in al-Musnad, 6:102 §24750, 24752.

[44] Al-Dhahabī in Kitāb al-Zuhd wa al-Ḥikma, p.165.

The Holy Prophet ﷺ did not speak a lot and he remained silent for long periods. According to Hind b. Abī Hāla ﵁:

كَانَ رَسُولُ اللهِ ﷺ لَا يَتَكَلَّمُ فِي غَيْرِ حَاجَةٍ، طَوِيلَ السَّكْتِ، يَفْتَتِحُ الْكَلَامَ وَيَخْتِمُهُ بِأَشْدَاقِهِ، وَيَتَكَلَّمُ بِجَوَامِعِ الْكَلِمِ، كَلَامُهُ فَصْلٌ لَا فُضُولٌ وَلَا تَقْصِيرٌ، لَيْسَ بِالْجَافِي وَلَا الْمُهِينِ.

> The Messenger of Allah ﷺ would not speak without need. He would maintain long periods of silence, and he would begin and end his speech clearly. He would speak with the most precise and comprehensive words. His speech was concise; it was neither excessive nor abridged, nor was it uncouth or contemptible.[45]

Al-Qāḍī ʿIyāḍ states:

وَكَانَ كَثِيرَ السُّكُوتِ، لَا يَتَكَلَّمُ فِي غَيْرِ حَاجَةٍ.

> The Holy Prophet ﷺ used to remain silent most of the time, and he would not talk unless it was necessary.[46]

Jābir b. Samra ﵁ states:

كَانَ رَسُولُ اللهِ ﷺ طَوِيلَ الصَّمْتِ.

> The Messenger of Allah ﷺ would remain silent for prolonged periods of time.[47]

On the importance of speaking less and on maintaining silence, Anas b. Mālik ﵁ relates that the Holy Prophet ﷺ said:

مَنْ سَرَّهُ أَنْ يَسْلَمَ فَلْيَلْزَمِ الصَّمْتَ.

---

[45] Narrated by al-Tirmidhī in *al-Shamāʾil al-Muḥammadiyya*, p.184-185 §226.

[46] Ibid., 1:275.

[47] Narrated by al-Bayhaqī in *al-Sunan al-Kubrā*, 10:240 §20,906 & 20,907.

Whoever wishes to be safe, let him maintain silence.⁴⁸

Sahl b. Sa'd ؓ relates that the Holy Prophet ﷺ said:

مَنْ يَضْمَنْ لِي مَا بَيْنَ لَحْيَيْهِ وَمَا بَيْنَ رِجْلَيْهِ أَضْمَنْ لَهُ الْجَنَّةَ.

Whoever guarantees what is between his jaw-bones and what is between his legs (i.e. the chastity of his tongue and private parts), I guarantee Paradise for him.⁴⁹

Abū Hurayra ؓ relates that the Holy Prophet ﷺ said:

مَنْ كَانَ يُؤْمِنُ بِاللهِ وَالْيَوْمِ الْآخِرِ فَلْيَقُلْ خَيْرًا أَوْ لِيَصْمُتْ.

Whoever believes in Allah ﷻ and the Last Day, let him say good or remain silent.⁵⁰

'Abd Allāh b. 'Amr ؓ relates that the Holy Prophet ﷺ said:

مَنْ صَمَتَ نَجَا.

Whoever maintains silence is saved.⁵¹

According to Imam Ibn Mājah, the Holy Prophet ﷺ said:

إِذَا رَأَيْتُمُ الرَّجُلَ قَدْ أُعْطِيَ زُهْدًا فِي الدُّنْيَا، وَقِلَّةَ مَنْطِقٍ، فَاقْتَرِبُوا مِنْهُ، فَإِنَّهُ يُلَقَّى الْحِكْمَةَ.

---

⁴⁸ Narrated by al-Bayhaqī in *al-Jāmi' al-Ṣaghīr*, 2:526 §8746.

⁴⁹ Narrated by al-Bukhārī in *al-Ṣaḥīḥ*: *Kitāb al-Riqāq* (The Book of Softening the Heart), chapter: 'Protecting one's tongue', 8:2189 §5476.

⁵⁰ Narrated by al-Bukhārī in *al-Ṣaḥīḥ*: *Kitāb al-Adab* (The Book of Etiquettes), chapter: 'Whoever believes in Allah ﷻ and the Last Day, let him not harm his neighbour', 8:11 §6018; and Muslim in *al-Ṣaḥīḥ*: *Kitāb al-Īmān* (The Book of Faith), chapter: 'The encouragement of honouring the neighbours and maintaining silence except in matters of goodness, and all of that being from faith', 1:68 §19.

⁵¹ Narrated by Aḥmad b. Ḥanbal in *al-Musnad*, 11:19 §6481.

> When you see a man who has been given abstinence from indulging in worldly desires and who speaks very little, then adopt his company for he is a man of wisdom.[52]

It is reported that Prophet ʿĪsā b. Maryam ﷺ said:

> أَقِلُّوا الْكَلَامَ إِلَّا مِنْ ذِكْرِ اللهِ، فَإِنَّ كَثْرَةَ الْكَلَامِ تُقَسِّي الْقَلْبَ.
>
> Decrease speech except in the remembrance of Allah ﷻ. For excessive speech hardens the heart.[53]

2.1.5 LISTENING TO SPIRITUAL AUDITIONS (SAMĀʿ)

The Holy Prophet ﷺ used to enjoy listening to the Holy Qur'ān, wholesome poetry and poetry in his praise (*madīḥ*). While listening to it he would enter into a state of divine attraction (*jadhb*) and longing (*shawq*). He used to arrange sittings solely for the purpose of listening to poetry, and he used to instruct Hassān b. Thābit ؓ to sing poetry in his presence. Sayyida ʿĀʾisha ؓ states in this regard:

> كَانَ رَسُولُ اللهِ ﷺ يَضَعُ لِحَسَّانَ مِنْبَرًا فِي الْمَسْجِدِ يَقُومُ عَلَيْهِ قَائِمًا يُفَاخِرُ عَنْ رَسُولِ اللهِ ﷺ- أَوْ قَالَتْ: يُنَافِحُ عَنْ رَسُولِ اللهِ ﷺ- وَيَقُولُ رَسُولُ اللهِ ﷺ: «إِنَّ اللهَ يُؤَيِّدُ حَسَّانَ بِرُوحِ الْقُدُسِ مَا يُفَاخِرُ، أَوْ يُنَافِحُ عَنْ رَسُولِ اللهِ».
>
> The Messenger of Allah ﷺ used to place a pulpit in the mosque for Ḥassān b. Thābit ؓ, upon which he would stand and praise the Messenger of Allah ﷺ; or she said: He would defend the Messenger of Allah ﷺ. The Messenger of Allah ﷺ would say, 'Allah has appointed Jibrīl to help Ḥassān while he praises the Messenger of Allah ﷺ; or (he said:) while he

---

[52] Narrated by Ibn Mājah in *al-Sunan*: *Kitāb al-Zuhd* [The Book of Abstinence], chapter: 'Abstinence in this world', 2:1373 §4101.

[53] Narrated by Abū Saʿd al-Nīsābūrī in *Tahdhīb al-Asrār*, p.451.

defends the Messenger of Allah ﷺ'.[54]

Ḥassān b. Thābit's poetry praising the Messenger of Allah ﷺ was full of love for the Holy Prophet ﷺ and it put people into a state of ecstasy. An example of it is given below:

وَأَحْسَنُ مِنْكَ لَمْ تَرَ قَطُّ عَيْنٌ
وَأَجْمَلُ مِنْكَ لَمْ تَلِدِ النِّسَاءُ
خُلِقْتَ مُبَرَّأً مِنْ كُلِّ عَيْبٍ
كَأَنَّكَ قَدْ خُلِقْتَ كَمَا تَشَاءُ

More beautiful than you, no eye has ever seen
Finer than you, no woman has given birth to
You have been created without any defect
As if you have been created as you wished

Likewise, on some occasions, the Holy Prophet ﷺ would also listen to the Companions reciting the Holy Qur'ān in melodious beautiful voices and would experience states of spiritual elation. The emotional and spiritual states that the Holy Prophet ﷺ would experience can be found in detail in books on *sīra* (the biography of the Holy Prophet ﷺ).

2.2 Principles of Sufism from the Practices of the Companions

All the principles of Sufism are practically seen in the lives of the Companions. They were trained directly by the Holy Prophet ﷺ in regard to the requirements of the spiritual path. The Holy Qur'ān mentions this connection and spiritual training:

﴿كَمَآ أَرۡسَلۡنَا فِيكُمۡ رَسُولٗا مِّنكُمۡ يَتۡلُواْ عَلَيۡكُمۡ ءَايَٰتِنَا
وَيُزَكِّيكُمۡ وَيُعَلِّمُكُمُ ٱلۡكِتَٰبَ وَٱلۡحِكۡمَةَ وَيُعَلِّمُكُم مَّا لَمۡ

[54] Narrated by al-Tirmidhī in *al-Sunan*: *Kitāb al-Adab* [The Book of Etiquettes], chapter: 'What has been related concerning reciting poetry', 5:138 §2846.

تَكُونُوا۟ تَعْلَمُونَ﴾

Likewise, We have sent you (Our) Messenger (blessings and peace be upon him) from amongst yourselves who recites to you Our Revelations and purifies and sanctifies (your hearts and ill-commanding selves) and teaches you the Book and inculcates in you logic and wisdom and enlightens you (on the mysteries of spiritual gnosis and divine truth) which you did not know.[55]

The correlation between the recitation of the verses and the purification of the lower self (*nafs*) is that the light of recitation enabled the Companions to be aware of their previous inner darkness. As each thing is defined relative to its opposite, when the light of recitation would manifest, and the Companions would be informed of the hidden illnesses of their lower selves (*nafs*), they would be concerned about carrying out a process of inner purification. As soon as the Companions desired internal purification, the Holy Prophet ﷺ directed their attention to their inner selves. When the hearts of the Companions became capable of becoming the vessels of divine light and the secrets of the Holy Qur'ān, then the Holy Prophet ﷺ would teach them the Holy Qur'ān and wisdom (*ḥikma*). This was the method of training through which the Companions through the help of their true guide and spiritual master, the Holy Prophet Muhammad ﷺ, excelled through the various grades of the spiritual path (*sulūk*).

The generations that followed the period of the Messenger of Allah ﷺ and his Companions focused largely on the external practices of the Sharia. These generations attained all the grades of the internal life through their observance of the rulings of the Sharia. Therefore, the *iḥsān*, or rather the attainment of *taṣawwuf*, of the early generations was through routine practices. They prayed the ritual prayer (*ṣalāh*); performed the remembrance of Allah (*dhikr*); recited the Holy Qur'ān; fasted; gave compulsory and voluntary charity; and partook in Jihad. There was not a single individual from amongst them who did not delve deep in the ocean of contemplation. These pious early generations did not strive through any other means than their deeds and their

55 Qur'ān 10:16.

remembrance of Allah (*dhikr*) to attain a strong relationship with Allah ﷻ.

Those who were great scholars from amongst these pious generations would gain pleasure from the ritual prayer (*ṣalāh*) and the remembrance of Allah (*dhikr*). They would be deeply moved by the recitation of the Holy Qur'ān. For example, they would not merely pay almsgiving (*zakāh*) because it was a commandment of Allah ﷻ, but alongside that they would perform it to purify themselves of stinginess and greed. Whenever they found themselves engrossed in worldly matters, they would pay the almsgiving (*zakāh*) and charity (*ṣadaqa*) in order to disconnect their hearts from worldly business. Likewise, they would have the same approach to the other commandments of the Sharia. They would not perform legally required acts merely considering them to be the commandments of Allah ﷻ, but they would perform them for the betterment and improvement of their inner selves.

Those states which result in supernatural occurrences and spiritual ecstasy were not so ingrained inside the Companions that it was a natural disposition. However, if anything manifested from them in this regard, then it was either of two cases: the first case was that when they sincerely believed in something with certainty, it would unintentionally manifest upon their tongues; the second case was that they would see certain things in their dreams, or they would understand the unknown through their intelligence. This was due to their pure inner selves or the blessing of their faith (*īmān*) that the impossible became possible.

There were, however, some Companions who used to engage in specific acts of additional worship and as a result they witnessed supernatural phenomena. They carried out practices that later came to be known as 'Sufi' practices. Some of those practices are discussed below.

2.2.1 Pledge of Allegiance (Bayʿa)

All of the Companions gave a pledge of allegiance (*bayʿa*) to the Holy Prophet ﷺ. There were many types of *bayʿa* that were performed with the Holy Prophet ﷺ:

1. The pledge to accept Islam (*bayʿa qubūl al-Islām*)
2. The pledge to the Caliph (*bayʿa al-khilāfa*)
3. The pledge to establish the injunctions of Islam (*bayʿa iqāma arkān al-dīn*)
4. The pledge to adhere to the Sunna and to be God-vigilant (*bayʿa al-tamassuk bi al-sunna wa al-taqwā*)
5. The pledge to abstain from innovation (*bayʿa al-ijtināb ʿan al-bidaʿ*)
6. The pledge to perform migration (*bayʿa al-hijra*)
7. The pledge to perform Jihad (*bayʿa al-jihād*)
8. The pledge of obedience (*bayʿa al-samʿ wa al-ṭāʿa*)
9. The pledge of love (*bayʿa al-maḥabba*)

The Sufi practice of *bayʿa* is no different from the above kinds of pledges that are established from the practice of the Companions. ʿUtba b. ʿAbd ﷺ stated:

بَايَعْتُ رَسُولَ اللهِ ﷺ سَبْعَ بَيْعَاتٍ خَمْسًا عَلَى الطَّاعَةِ وَاثْنَتَيْنِ عَلَى الْمَحَبَّةِ.

> I pledged allegiance to the Holy Prophet ﷺ on seven different occasions; five to pledge my obedience and two to pledge my love.[56]

Abū Nuʿaym and Ibn ʿĀsākir narrate that Anas b. Mālik ﷺ stated:

بَايَعْتُ النَّبِيَّ ﷺ بِيَدِي هَذِهِ عَلَى السَّمْعِ وَالطَّاعَةِ فِيمَا اسْتَطَعْتُ.

> I pledged allegiance to the Holy Prophet ﷺ with this hand of mine to obey him to the best of my abilities.[57]

It is established from the above narrations that during the period of the Holy Prophet ﷺ and the Companions, the *bayʿa* was not only confined to giving an oath of allegiance to the ruler or on embracing Islam, rather it was established for a number of different matters.

---

[56] Narrated by al-Hindī in *Kanz al-ʿUmmāl*, 1:172 §1524.

[57] Narrated by al-Kāndahlawī in *Ḥayāt al-Ṣaḥāba*, 1:298.

Shāh Walī Allāh Muḥaddith al-Dihlawī states in relation to the *bayʿa*:

فَاعْلَمْ أَنَّ الْبَيْعَةَ سُنَّةٌ وَلَيْسَتْ بِوَاجِبَةٍ لِأَنَّ النَّاسَ بَايَعُوا النَّبِيَّ ﷺ وَتَقَرَّبُوا بِهَا إِلَى اللهِ تَعَالَى.

> Know that *bayʿa* is Sunna and not compulsory (*wājib*). The Companions used to perform *bayʿa* with the Holy Prophet ﷺ and would acquire closeness to Allah ﷻ through it.[58]

There are two points understood from this explanation by Shāh Walī Allāh Muḥaddith al-Dihlawī. Firstly, that performing *bayʿa* is Sunna and not an innovation (*bidʿa*). Secondly, that performing *bayʿa* is a means of attaining Allah's nearness.

2.2.2 KEEPING THE COMPANY OF A SPIRITUAL GUIDE (ṢUḤBA)

The Holy Qur'ān specifically mentions the company kept by the Companions. Allah ﷻ says:

﴿مُّحَمَّدٌ رَّسُولُ ٱللَّهِۚ وَٱلَّذِينَ مَعَهُۥٓ أَشِدَّآءُ عَلَى ٱلْكُفَّارِ رُحَمَآءُ بَيْنَهُمْۖ تَرَىٰهُمْ رُكَّعًا سُجَّدًا يَبْتَغُونَ فَضْلًا مِّنَ ٱللَّهِ وَرِضْوَٰنًاۖ﴾

> *Muhammad (ﷺ) is the Messenger of Allah. And those with him are hard and tough against the disbelievers but kind-hearted and merciful amongst themselves. You see them excessively bowing and prostrating themselves. They simply seek Allah's grace and pleasure.*[59]

The Companions were very much aware of the etiquettes of being in the company of their most perfect spiritual master and guide, the Holy Prophet ﷺ. They showed the utmost respect, honour and reverence towards him.

Abū Juḥayfa ؓ narrated:

---

58 Shāh Walī Allāh, *al-Qawl al-Jamīl*, p.18.

59 Qur'ān 48:29.

> خَرَجَ عَلَيْنَا رَسُولُ اللهِ ﷺ بِالْهَاجِرَةِ، فَأُتِيَ بِوَضُوءٍ فَتَوَضَّأَ، فَجَعَلَ النَّاسُ يَأْخُذُونَ مِنْ فَضْلِ وَضُوئِهِ فَيَتَمَسَّحُونَ بِهِ.

The Holy Prophet ﷺ came out to where we were. Then he was given water to perform ablution (*wuḍūʾ*). He performed ablution (*wuḍūʾ*) and people took the left-over water and rubbed it upon themselves (on their eyes and faces).[60]

In another narration, Sāʾib b. Yazīd ؓ says:

> ذَهَبَتْ بِي خَالَتِي إِلَى النَّبِيِّ ﷺ فَقَالَتْ: يَا رَسُولَ اللهِ، إِنَّ ابْنَ أُخْتِي وَقِعٌ، فَمَسَحَ رَأْسِي، وَدَعَا لِي بِالْبَرَكَةِ، ثُمَّ تَوَضَّأَ، فَشَرِبْتُ مِنْ وَضُوئِهِ.

My maternal aunt took me to the Holy Prophet ﷺ and said: "O Messenger of Allah ﷺ, this is my nephew; he has fallen ill." The Holy Prophet ﷺ wiped my head with his hand and supplicated for me to receive an increase in bestowed blessings (*baraka*). Then he performed ablution (*wuḍūʾ*) and I drank the leftover water.[61]

The Companions used to kiss the hands and feet of the Holy Prophet ﷺ in order to gain blessings. It was also a mark of utmost respect and reverence. Wāziʿ b. ʿĀmir, who is popularly known as Wāziʿ al-ʿAbdī, said:

> قَدِمْنَا فَقِيلَ: ذَاكَ رَسُولُ اللهِ ﷺ، فَأَخَذْنَا بِيَدَيْهِ وَرِجْلَيْهِ نُقَبِّلُهَا.

We came to see the Holy Prophet ﷺ, and it was said to us, 'That is the Messenger of Allah.' So, we held his hands and feet and kissed them.[62]

---

[60] Narrated by al-Bukhārī in *al-Ṣaḥīḥ*: *Kitāb al-Wuḍūʾ* [The Book on the Ritual Ablution], chapter: 'Using the left-over ablution water', 1:80 §185.

[61] Narrated by al-Bukhārī in *al-Ṣaḥīḥ*: *Kitāb al-Wuḍūʾ* [The Book on the Ritual Ablution], chapter: 'Using the left-over ablution water', 1:81 §186.

[62] Narrated by al-Bukhārī in *al-Adab al-Mufrad*, 1:339 §975.

Imam Abū Dāwūd narrates that Zāriʿ said:

لَمَّا قَدِمْنَا الْمَدِينَةَ فَجَعَلْنَا نَتَبَادَرُ مِنْ رَوَاحِلِنَا، فَنُقَبِّلُ يَدَ النَّبِيِّ ﷺ وَرِجْلَهُ.

> We came to Madina, and we rushed off our rides so that we could kiss the hands and feet of the Holy Prophet ﷺ.[63]

It was the case that those Companions whose hands had touched the Holy Prophet ﷺ that other Companions and Successors would kiss their hands and stand up for them out of respect.[64]

The Companions used to give gifts and presents to the Holy Prophet ﷺ as a mark of love and respect. The Holy Prophet ﷺ used to accept them and also used to give gifts to the Companions.

On the importance of keeping good company, Abū Saʿīd ؓ narrates that the Messenger of Allah ﷺ said:

لَا تُصَاحِبْ إِلَّا مُؤْمِنًا، وَلَا يَأْكُلْ طَعَامَكَ إِلَّا تَقِيٌّ.

> Do not accompany anyone except a believer, and do not serve your food to anyone except to one with *taqwā*.[65]

Abū Hurayra ؓ narrates that the Holy Prophet ﷺ said:

اَلرَّجُلُ عَلَى دِينِ خَلِيلِهِ، فَلْيَنْظُرْ أَحَدُكُمْ مَنْ يُخَالِلُ.

> A man is upon the religion of his friend. So let him consider whom he takes as a friend.[66]

---

63 Narrated by Abū Dāwūd in *al-Sunan*: *Kitāb al-Adab* [The Book of Etiquettes], chapter: 'Kissing the body', 4:357 §5225.

64 Narrated by al-Bukhārī in *al-Adab al-Mufrad*, 1:338 §973.

65 Narrated by al-Tirmidhī in *al-Sunan*: *Abwāb al-Zuhd* [The Chapters on Renunciation], chapter: 'On the Companionship of the believer', 4:600 §2395.

66 Narrated Abū Dāwūd in *al-Sunan*: *Kitāb al-Adab* [The Book of Etiquettes], chapter: 'The one with whom it is commanded to associate', 4:259 §4833.

Asmā' bint Yazīd ؓ narrates that she heard the Messenger of Allah ﷺ say:

أَلَا أُنَبِّئُكُمْ بِخِيَارِكُمْ؟ قَالُوا: بَلَى يَا رَسُولَ اللهِ. قَالَ: خِيَارُكُمُ الَّذِينَ إِذَا رُءُوا ذُكِرَ اللهُ.

"Shall I not tell you of the best of you?" The Companions said: "Yes, O Messenger of Allah ﷺ." He ﷺ said: "The best amongst you are those who, when they are seen, Allah ﷻ is remembered."[67]

Ibn ʿAbbās ؓ narrates:

قِيلَ: يَا رَسُولَ اللهِ، مَنْ أَوْلِيَاءُ اللهِ؟ قَالَ: اَلَّذِينَ إِذَا رُءُوا ذُكِرَ اللهُ.

It was asked: "O Messenger of Allah ﷺ, who are the friends of Allah?" He ﷺ said: "Those who, when they are seen, Allah ﷻ is remembered."[68]

ʿAmr b. al-Jamūḥ ؓ narrates that he heard the Messenger of Allah ﷺ say:

قَالَ اللهُ تَعَالَى: إِنَّ أَوْلِيَائِي مِنْ عِبَادِي وَأَحِبَّائِي مِنْ خَلْقِي الَّذِينَ يُذْكَرُونَ بِذِكْرِي وَأُذْكَرُ بِذِكْرِهِمْ.

Allah Almighty said: "Verily, My intimate friends amongst My beloved servants from My creation are those who are remembered through My remembrance and I am remembered through their remembrance."[69]

On the type of friends one should keep, ʿUthmān b. Ḥakīm said:

---

67 Narrated by Ibn Mājah in *al-Sunan*: *Kitāb al-Zuhd* [The Book of Renunciation], chapter: 'The one to whom no one pays attention', 2:1379 §4119.

68 Narrated by al-Ḥakīm al-Tirmidhī, *Nawādir al-Uṣūl*, 2:39.

69 Ibid., 2:41.

اِصْحَبْ مَنْ هُوَ فَوْقَكَ فِي الدِّينِ، وَمَنْ هُوَ دُونَكَ فِي الدُّنْيَا، فَإِنَّ صُحْبَةَ مَنْ فَوْقَكَ فِي الدِّينِ تُصَغِّرُ فِي نَفْسِكَ طَاعَاتِكَ، وَصُحْبَةَ مَنْ دُونَكَ فِي الدُّنْيَا تُعَظِّمُ فِي عَيْنِكَ نِعَمَ اللهِ تَعَالَى.

Adopt the company of one who is above you in religion and lesser than you in the world. For adopting the company of the one above you in religion will make your worship feel insignificant in yourself, while adopting the company of the one lesser than you in the world will enhance the greatness of Allah's blessings in your eyes.[70]

2.2.3 SITTINGS OF REMEMBRANCE AND REFLECTION (MAJĀLIS AL-DHIKR WA AL-FIKR)

In the time of the Holy Prophet ﷺ and the Companions, it was an established practice to hold regular gatherings for the remembrance of Allah (*dhikr*) and reflection (*fikr*). Sometimes in these gatherings, people used to reach spiritual states such as spiritual unveiling and witnessing (*mukāshāfa*). The Companion Ḥanzala al-Usaydī رضي الله عنه complained to the Holy Prophet ﷺ about the lack of continuity of the spiritual state that he used to experience during these gatherings of remembrance (*dhikr*) and reflection (*fikr*). The Holy Prophet ﷺ said:

لَوْ كَانَتْ تَكُونُ قُلُوبُكُمْ كَمَا تَكُونُ عِنْدَ الذِّكْرِ، لَصَافَحَتْكُمُ الْمَلَائِكَةُ، حَتَّى تُسَلِّمَ عَلَيْكُمْ فِي الطُّرُقِ.

If your hearts continue to remain in that spiritual state as they are during the time of *dhikr*, then the angels would shake hands with you and even greet you in the streets.[71]

---

[70] Al-Sulamī, *Kitāb al-Futuwwa*.

[71] Narrated by Muslim in *al-Ṣaḥīḥ*: *Kitāb al-Tawba* [The Book of Repentance], chapter: 'The excellence of continuing remembrance (*dhikr*), contemplation in the matters of the Hereafter and meditation, and the permissibility to leave them at certain times to occupy oneself with the matters of this world', 4:2107 §2750.

Imam al-Nawawī writes in his commentary of *Ṣaḥīḥ Muslim*:

يَظْهَرُ عَلَيْهِ ذَلِكَ مَعَ الْمُرَاقَبَةِ وَالْفِكْرِ وَالْإِقْبَالِ عَلَى الْآخِرَةِ.

> This spiritual state manifests through meditation (*murāqaba*), reflection (*fikr*) and by paying attention to the Hereafter.[72]

It is stated in *Ṣaḥīḥ al-Bukhārī* that ʿAbd Allāh b. Masʿūd ﷺ used to hold a *dhikr* circle every Thursday.[73] The Sufis generally adopt this practice of ʿAbd Allāh b. Masʿūd ﷺ.

Shaykh ʿAbd al-Qādir al-Jīlānī states that Angel Jibrīl ﷺ instructed the Holy Prophet ﷺ to perform the *dhikr* of negation and affirmation (i.e. *Lā ilāha illā Allāh*). The Holy Prophet ﷺ trained ʿAlī ﷺ upon this and likewise all of the Companions were taught about this.[74]

According to Shaykh Aḥmad al-Rifāʿī, the Holy Prophet ﷺ taught ʿAlī ﷺ how to perform the *dhikr* of negation and affirmation (i.e. *Lā ilāha illā Allāh*) by closing the eyes and performing it loudly.[75]

Shaykh Aḥmad al-Rifāʿī also quotes this narration:

فَقَالَ ﷺ: أَغْمِضْ عَيْنَيْكَ وَاسْمَعْ مِنِّي ثَلَاثَ مَرَّاتٍ، ثُمَّ قُلْ أَنْتَ ثَلَاثَ مَرَّاتٍ، وَأَنَا أَسْمَعُ. فَقَالَ: لَا إِلَهَ إِلَّا اللهُ ثَلَاثَ مَرَّاتٍ، مُغْمِضًا عَيْنَيْهِ رَافِعًا صَوْتَهُ.

> The Holy Prophet ﷺ said to ʿAlī ﷺ, "Close your eyes and listen to me reciting it three times. Then you recite it three times and I will listen. Then ʿAlī ﷺ recited '*Lā ilāha illā Allāh*' three times loudly with his eyes closed."[76]

---

72 Al-Nawawī, *Sharḥ Ṣaḥīḥ Muslim*, 17:66.

73 Narrated by al-Bukhārī in *al-Ṣaḥīḥ*: *Kitāb al-ʿIlm* [The Book of Knowledge], chapter: 'On the one who appointed fixed days for the people desiring knowledge', 1:39 §70.

74 ʿAbd al-Qādir al-Jīlānī, *Sirr al-Asrār*, p.68.

75 Aḥmad al-Rifāʿī, *al-Burhān al-Muʾayyad*, p.53–54.

76 Ibid., p.63.

'Abd Allāh b. 'Abbās ؓ states:

$$\text{أَنَّ رَفْعَ الصَّوْتِ بِالذِّكْرِ حِينَ يَنْصَرِفُ النَّاسُ مِنَ الْمَكْتُوبَةِ كَانَ عَلَى عَهْدِ النَّبِيِّ ﷺ.}$$

Raising the voice in *dhikr* after the completion of the obligatory (*farḍ*) prayer was a practice during the time of the Holy Prophet ﷺ."[77]

2.2.4 VISUALISATION OF THE SPIRITUAL GUIDE (TAṢAWWUR AL-SHAYKH)

The Companions used to imagine or visualise in their minds the spiritual guide of the two worlds, the Holy Prophet ﷺ. They would gain spiritual contentment and blessings from it. Abū Mūsā al-Ashʿarī ؓ stated:

$$\text{وَكَأَنِّي أَنْظُرُ إِلَى سِوَاكِهِ تَحْتَ شَفَتِهِ.}$$

It is as though I can see his toothbrush (*siwak*) under his lips.[78]

ʿAmr b. Ḥurayth ؓ stated:

$$\text{كَأَنِّي أَنْظُرُ إِلَى رَسُولِ اللهِ ﷺ عَلَى الْمِنْبَرِ، وَعَلَيْهِ عِمَامَةٌ سَوْدَاءُ.}$$

It is as though I am visualising him sitting upon the pulpit, wearing a black turban with both of its ends hanging between the back of his shoulders.[79]

The importance of this concept can be gauged by the fact that Imam

---

[77] Narrated by al-Bukhārī in *al-Ṣaḥīḥ*: *Kitāb Ṣifa al-Ṣalāt* [The Book on the Description of the Ritual Prayer], chapter: 'Dhikr after the ritual prayer', 1:288 §805.

[78] Narrated by Muslim in *al-Ṣaḥīḥ*: *Kitāb al-Imāra* [The Book of Emirate], chapter: 'The prohibition of seeking and desiring power and authority', 3:1456 §1733.

[79] Narrated by Muslim in *al-Ṣaḥīḥ*: *Kitāb al-Imāra* [The Book of Emirate], chapter: 'The permission of entering Makkah without the pilgrim's attire (*iḥrām*)', 2:992 §1359.

al-Ghazālī instructs people to create this state of mind during the ritual prayer. He states:

وَأَحْضِرْ فِي قَلْبِكَ النَّبِيَّ ﷺ وَشَخْصَهُ الْكَرِيمَ وَقُلْ سَلَامٌ عَلَيْكَ أَيُّهَا النَّبِيُّ.

> Present the Holy Prophet ﷺ in your heart and [visualise] his venerable person and say: '*Salām ʿalayka ayyuhā al-Nabī*' (Greetings be upon you, O Prophet!).[80]

In relation to this visualisation during the ritual prayer (*ṣalāh*), Imam al-ʿAsqalānī in *Fatḥ al-Bārī* and Mawlānā Shabbīr Aḥmad ʿUthmānī in *Fatḥ al-Mulhim* have penned very interesting discussions which are worth studying. The Sufis have taken this practice of the Companions as a precedent and have adopted the practice of visualising one's spiritual guide (*shaykh*).

2.2.5 Woollen Clothes

Many Companions used to wear a rough woollen dress. In his *al-Muṣannaf*, Imam Ibn Abī Shayba relates a report from ʿUmayr b. Isḥāq ﵁, who relates that the Messenger of Allah ﷺ said on the day of the Battle of Badr:

تَسَوَّمُوا، فَإِنَّ الْمَلَائِكَةَ قَدْ تَسَوَّمَتْ. قَالُوا: فَأَوَّلُ مَا جُعِلَ الصُّوفُ لِيَوْمَئِذٍ.

> Adopt a symbol (i.e., a distinguishing mark by which one is known), for the angels have adopted a symbol. They said: "It was since that day that wool was adopted as a symbol."[81]

Imam Ḥasan al-Baṣrī states:

لَقَدْ أَدْرَكْتُ سَبْعِينَ بَدْرِيًّا كَانَ لِبَاسُهُمُ الصُّوفَ.

---

[80] Al-Ghazālī, *Iḥyā' ʿUlūm al-Dīn*, 1:169.

[81] Narrated by Ibn Abī Shayba in *al-Muṣannaf*, 6:437 §32,722.

> I have met seventy veterans of the Battle of Badr, and their garment was nothing but wool.[82]

Evidently, Imam Ḥasan al-Baṣrī had not been born in that time to witness the Battle of Badr. Nevertheless, recounting his meetings with the veterans, he mentions that they used to wear garments made from wool.

In this vein, Sayyidunā ʿAlī b. Abī Ṭālib ﷺ relates:

كَانَ سِيمَا أَصْحَابِ رَسُولِ اللهِ يَوْمَ بَدْرٍ الصُّوفُ الْأَبْيَضُ.

> The hallmark of the Companions of Allah's Messenger ﷺ on the Day of Badr was white cotton.[83]

Imam al-Khāzin in his exegesis relates regarding Salmān al-Fārisī's woollen clothing:

وَعِنْدَهُ جَمَاعَةٌ مِنَ الْفُقَرَاءِ وَمِنْهُمْ سَلْمَانُ وَعَلَيْهِ صُوفٌ.

> There was a group of dervishes (*fuqarā'*) with him and Salmān al-Fārisī was also among them. He was wearing a woollen cloak (*ṣūf*).[84]

2.2.6 THE COMPANIONS OF THE VERANDA (AṢḤĀB AL-ṢUFFA) – THE FIRST GROUP OF SUFIS

The Companions of the Veranda (*Aṣḥāb al-Ṣuffa*) were the first organised group of Sufis. They gave priority to spiritual training over worldly matters and remained with the Holy Prophet ﷺ on a continual basis and advanced in the various grades of *taṣawwuf*. Regarding them, Allah ﷻ states in the Holy Qur'ān:

﴿وَلَا تَطْرُدِ ٱلَّذِينَ يَدْعُونَ رَبَّهُم بِٱلْغَدَوٰةِ وَٱلْعَشِيِّ يُرِيدُونَ

---

82 Mullā ʿAlī al-Qārī, *Mirqāt al-Mafātīḥ*, 8:193; al-Aṣbahānī, *Ḥilya al-Awliyā'*, 2:134; and al-Kalābādhī, *al-Taʿarruf li Madhhab Ahl al-Taṣawwuf*, p.23.

83 Narrated by Ibn Abī Shayba in *al-Muṣannaf*, 6:437 §32,723.

84 Al-Khāzin, *Lubāb al-Ta'wīl*, 4:209.

﴿وَجْهَهُ﴾

And do not turn away these (run-down and broken-hearted) people (from your company and close circle) who call upon their Lord persistently, seeking only His pleasure morning and evening.[85]

And at another place, it is stated:

﴿لِلْفُقَرَآءِ ٱلَّذِينَ أُحْصِرُوا۟ فِى سَبِيلِ ٱللَّهِ لَا يَسْتَطِيعُونَ ضَرْبًا فِى ٱلْأَرْضِ يَحْسَبُهُمُ ٱلْجَاهِلُ أَغْنِيَآءَ مِنَ ٱلتَّعَفُّفِ تَعْرِفُهُم بِسِيمَٰهُمْ﴾

(Charity is) the right of those poor who have been restricted (from earning their livelihood) in the cause of Allah. They cannot even move about in the land (due to their whole-time involvement in matters of Din [Religion]). Because of their (ascetic) aversion to greed, the unwise (knowing little about their state of heart and soul) consider them wealthy. You will recognise them from their appearance.[86]

The Companions of the Veranda (*Aṣḥāb al-Ṣuffa*) lived in the courtyard of *Masjid al-Nabawī* and were continually engaged in the purification of the lower self (*nafs*). Their number is proven to be between seventy to seven hundred, as some narrations have mentioned over seventy, while others mention one hundred, while others even state that seven hundred Companions used to come and stay there at a time. The common attribute among them all was that they ate less and remained unmarried during their stay there.

Imam al-Tirmidhī narrates in *Jāmiʿ al-Tirmidhī* regarding eating less:

كَانَ إِذَا صَلَّى بِالنَّاسِ يَخِرُّ رِجَالٌ مِنْ قَامَتِهِمْ فِي الصَّلَاةِ مِنَ الْخَصَاصَةِ وَهُمْ أَصْحَابُ الصُّفَّةِ حَتَّى تَقُولَ الْأَعْرَابُ هَؤُلَاءِ

---

[85] Qur'ān 6:52.

[86] Qur'ān 2:273.

مَجَانِينُ أَوْ مَجَانُونَ. فَإِذَا صَلَّى رَسُولُ اللهِ ﷺ انْصَرَفَ إِلَيْهِمْ، فَقَالَ: «لَوْ تَعْلَمُونَ مَا لَكُمْ عِنْدَ اللهِ لَأَحْبَبْتُمْ أَنْ تَزْدَادُوا فَاقَةً وَحَاجَةً».

> When the Holy Prophet ﷺ would be leading the prayer, many individuals from the Companions of the Veranda (*Aṣḥāb al-Ṣuffa*) would collapse due to weakness from hunger. The Bedouins would see them and say, "These people are mental." After completing the prayer, the Holy Prophet ﷺ would address the Companions of the Veranda and say to them, "If you knew the reward that Allah ﷻ has for you, you would want to increase your hunger and your poverty."[87]

Imam al-Ṣāwī and ʿAllāma Shiblī al-Nuʿmānī state regarding the Companions of the Veranda (*Aṣḥāb al-Ṣuffa*) not getting married:

> They had devoted their lives in worship and in being educated and spiritually trained by the Holy Prophet ﷺ. They did not have wives or children and when they got married, they would leave the company of the veranda.[88]

The Companions of the Veranda (*Aṣḥāb al-Ṣuffa*) remaining celibate brings to light the reality that those Sufis who remained celibate and refrained from worldly matters in order to elevate their spirituality, did not violate Islamic teachings or commit an innovation (*bidʿa*). In fact, the view of Islam is that if a group of organised individuals want to spend all their time in internal purification, then they would be following the practice of the Companions of the Veranda (*Aṣḥāb al-Ṣuffa*). This practice of theirs cannot be termed as monasticism (*rahbāniya*), which is forbidden in Islam.

The system practised by the Companions of the Veranda (*Aṣḥāb al-Ṣuffa*) was adopted by Sufis in Sufi retreats (*zāwiya/khānqāh*) which sadly do not exist anymore.

---

[87] Narrated by al-Tirmidhī in *al-Sunan*: *Kitāb al-Zuhd* [The Book of Abstinence], chapter: 'What has been related concerning the livelihood of the Companions of the Holy Prophet ﷺ, 4:583 §2368.

[88] Al-Ṣāwī, *Ḥāshiya*, 1:130; and Shiblī al-Nuʿmānī, *Sīra al-Nabī* ﷺ, 1:271.

Some examples of *taṣawwuf* and *iḥsān* have been presented from the lives of the Companions. In truth, every moment of their lives was *taṣawwuf* and *iḥsān*. The hidden truths (*maʿārif*) of *taṣawwuf* came into being from their utterances and the subtle inner capacities (*laṭāʾif*) of the reality came into being from their states and inclinations.

3

THE FIVE FUNDAMENTAL REQUIREMENTS OF SUFISM

In Sufism (*taṣawwuf*), there are two different paths for the seeker (*sālik*) to reach the desired destination. The first is *sulūk* (spiritual wayfaring) and the other is *jadhb* (divine attraction). In the former, the seeker adopts *sulūk*, where he or she travels upon the spiritual path to attain Allah's nearness; this path is arduous and requires spiritual effort and hardwork. In the latter, the person is known as *majdhūb* as he or she is chosen by Allah ﷻ and experiences divine attraction without striving. In the Qur'ān, Allah ﷻ states:

﴿ٱللَّهُ يَجْتَبِيٓ إِلَيْهِ مَن يَشَآءُ وَيَهْدِيٓ إِلَيْهِ مَن يُنِيبُ﴾

Allah chooses whom He pleases (for exclusive nearness) in His presence and shows the path to (come) towards Himself to everyone who turns (towards Allah) heartily.[89]

Sufism (*taṣawwuf*) is fundamentally based upon *sulūk* (spiritual wayfaring), which is why its requirements will be discussed. There are no set rules for *jadhb* (divine attraction). *Sulūk* has five initial

[89] Qur'ān 42:13.

fundamental requirements, without which a seeker (*sālik*) on the path of Sufism (*taṣawwuf*) cannot begin the journey nor progress. They are:

1. Acquiring knowledge (*ʿilm*) and obedience to God (*taqwā*)
2. Following a spiritual master (*Shaykh*)
3. Limiting food, sleep and speech
4. Abundant remembrance of Allah (*dhikr*) and worship (*ʿibāda*)
5. Contemplation (*tafakkur*) and meditation (*murāqaba*)

A seeker (*sālik*) cannot reach the required destination if these five requirements are not adhered to. For this reason, these initial five requirements will be discussed in more detail.

The Sufis ascertain these five requirements from the following verse:

﴿يَٰٓأَيُّهَا ٱلَّذِينَ ءَامَنُواْ ٱتَّقُواْ ٱللَّهَ وَٱبۡتَغُوٓاْ إِلَيۡهِ ٱلۡوَسِيلَةَ وَجَٰهِدُواْ
فِي سَبِيلِهِۦ لَعَلَّكُمۡ تُفۡلِحُونَ﴾

O believers! Fear Allah persistently and keep looking for means to (approach and get closer to) Him and strive hard in His way so that you may prosper.[90]

This verse mentions four things: faith (*īmān*), vigilance to the commands of Allah (*taqwā*), intermediation (*wasīla*) and striving (*jihād*); and, according to this verse, their combined outcome is prosperity and success (*falāḥ*).

In the verse, faith (*īmān*) is an indication to the first requirement, which is to acquire knowledge (*ʿilm*) and obedience to God. Vigilance to the commands of Allah (*taqwā*) is an indication towards striving to abide by the divine injunctions. Intermediation (*wasīla*), i.e. striving for a means, is an indication towards following a spiritual master (*shaykh*). Whereas striving (*jihād*) is an indication to the last three requirements of: (1) limiting food, sleep and speech; (2) abundant remembrance of Allah (*dhikr*) and worship (*ʿibāda*); (3) and contemplation (*tafakkur*) and meditation (*murāqaba*) – in the hadith, this is referred to as the 'greater struggle' (*al-jihād al-akbar*), i.e., (*jihād*

---

90 Qur'ān 5:35.

bi al-nafs). The outcome of all of these things is 'prosperity and success' (*falāḥ*), which indicates that the seeker (*sālik*) cannot progress on the spiritual path without these five fundamental requirements.

3.1 Acquiring Knowledge (ʿIlm) and Obedience to God (Taqwā)

The requirement to attain knowledge and to practise upon it is clear from the verse of the Holy Qur'ān:

﴿يَرْفَعِ ٱللَّهُ ٱلَّذِينَ ءَامَنُوا۟ مِنكُمْ وَٱلَّذِينَ أُوتُوا۟ ٱلْعِلْمَ دَرَجَـٰتٍ ۚ وَٱللَّهُ بِمَا تَعْمَلُونَ خَبِيرٌ﴾

Allah will raise those in ranks who believe from amongst you and who are given knowledge. And Allah is Well Aware of the works that you do.[91]

The foundation and basis of Sufism (*taṣawwuf*) is the Sharia, and the primary requirement of the Sharia is faith and practice. The Sharia regards faith and practice to be the sole means of deliverance from the punishment of the hereafter. Time and again it is stated in the Holy Qur'ān:

﴿إِلَّا ٱلَّذِينَ ءَامَنُوا۟ وَعَمِلُوا۟ ٱلصَّـٰلِحَـٰتِ﴾

Except those who believed and performed good deeds.[92]

Faith (*īmān*) and practice upon the teachings of Islam (*ʿamal*) cannot be separated from each other. Faith can be described as being based wholly upon knowledge, while practice as being based wholly upon obedience.

Without knowledge (*ʿilm*), it is not possible to attain true faith (*īmān*), as belief in the Divine Oneness (*tawḥīd*) and the Messengership (*risāla*) is predicated on knowledge. Likewise, without knowledge, it is

91 Qur'ān 58:11.

92 Qur'ān 103:3.

not possible to implement the pillars of Islam in one's life, or to know what the obligations, recommendations and prohibitions are. Thus, it is not possible to attain faith (*īmān*) without knowledge. For this reason, the acquisition of beneficial knowledge has been made obligatory, as commanded by the Messenger of Allah ﷺ:

طَلَبُ الْعِلْمِ فَرِيضَةٌ عَلَى كُلِّ مُسْلِمٍ.

Acquiring knowledge is an obligation on every Muslim.[93]

Knowledge is essential to function in this world, and there is no excuse for not acquiring obligatory knowledge. After knowing and believing in the commandments of Allah ﷻ, obedience to Allah ﷻ and His Messenger ﷺ becomes obligatory. The main purpose of raising the Prophets is that they are followed and obeyed. Allah ﷻ states in the Holy Qur'ān:

﴿وَمَآ أَرْسَلْنَا مِن رَّسُولٍ إِلَّا لِيُطَاعَ بِإِذْنِ ٱللَّهِ﴾

We have not sent any Messenger but that he must be obeyed by the command of Allah.[94]

Obedience to the Messenger ﷺ has been declared obedience to Allah ﷻ. It is further stated in the Holy Qur'ān:

﴿مَّن يُطِعِ ٱلرَّسُولَ فَقَدْ أَطَاعَ ٱللَّهَ﴾

Whoever obeys the Messenger ﷺ obeys (but) Allah indeed.[95]

It is not possible to obey the Holy Messenger ﷺ without the knowledge of the Sunna, without which it is impossible to follow the Sufi path (*sulūk*). Allah ﷻ states in the Holy Qur'ān:

---

[93] Narrated by Ibn Mājah in *al-Sunan*: *Muqaddima* [Preface], chapter: 'The virtue of the scholars, and encouragement to seek knowledge', 1:81 §224.

[94] Qur'ān 4:64.

[95] Qur'ān 4:80.

﴿قُلْ إِن كُنتُمْ تُحِبُّونَ ٱللَّهَ فَٱتَّبِعُونِى يُحْبِبْكُمُ ٱللَّهُ﴾

(O Beloved!) Say: 'If you love Allah, follow me. Allah will then take you as (His) beloved.[96]

Loving God is the ultimate aim in the Sufi path (*sulūk*). The primary condition for achieving this is obedience to the Holy Prophet ﷺ. Once this obedience to the Holy Prophet ﷺ has been fulfilled, then divine attention is gained as a result. Attaining divine attention is the essence of *taṣawwuf*. For this reason, before stepping upon this path, it is essential to acquire knowledge of the Holy Qur'ān and Sunna. An ignorant worshipper cannot successfully complete the first stage of the spiritual path, even if he spends his whole life in the worship of Allah ﷻ. The Holy Prophet ﷺ stated:

فَقِيهٌ وَاحِدٌ أَشَدُّ عَلَى الشَّيْطَانِ مِنْ أَلْفِ عَابِدٍ.

A single jurist (*faqīh*) is harder on Satan (to misguide) than a thousand worshippers.[97]

Imam Mālik famously said:

مَنْ تَفَقَّهَ وَلَمْ يَتَصَوَّفْ فَقَدْ تَفَسَّقَ، وَمَنْ تَصَوَّفَ وَلَمْ يَتَفَقَّهْ فَقَدْ تَزَنْدَقَ، وَمَنْ جَمَعَ بَيْنَهُمَا فَقَدْ تَحَقَّقَ.

Whoever studied the law (i.e. *fiqh*) but did not study *taṣawwuf* will be corrupted; and whoever studied *taṣawwuf* and did not study the law (i.e. *fiqh*) will become a heretic; and whoever combined both will attain the Truth.[98]

The Sufi elders have said:

---

96 Qur'ān 3:31.

97 Narrated by Ibn Mājah in *al-Sunan*: *Muqaddima* [Preface], chapter: 'The virtue of the scholars, and encouragement to seek knowledge', 1:81 §222; and al-Ṭabarānī in *al-Muʿjam al-Kabīr*, 11:78 §11,099.

98 Mullā ʿAlī al-Qārī, *Mirqāt al-Mafātīḥ*, 1:478.

فَلَا تَصَوُّفَ إِلَّا بِفِقْهٍ إِذْ لَا تُعْرَفُ أَحْكَامُ اللهِ تَعَالَى الظَّاهِرَةُ إِلَّا مِنْهُ.

There is no Sufism except through the study of the law (i.e. *fiqh*), as it is not possible to know the apparent rulings of Allah ﷻ except by it.[99]

Therefore, it is clear that without acquiring the knowledge of the Sharia, it is impossible to save oneself from the punishment in the hereafter, let alone gain the gnosis of Almighty Allah. After attaining the knowledge of the Sharia, it is necessary to bring into practice that knowledge in order to excel in obedience. The punishment on the Day of Judgement for a scholar who does not practise the acquired knowledge is to have the tongue cut off by scissors made out of fire. It is stated in the Holy Qur'ān:

﴿كَبُرَ مَقْتًا عِندَ ٱللَّهِ أَن تَقُولُوا۟ مَا لَا تَفْعَلُونَ﴾

It is most hateful in the sight of Allah that you should say what you do not do.[100]

The example of a scholar who does not practise the teachings of Islam is that of a donkey that has been loaded with a heavy load of books. A seeker or traveller on the path of God must gain knowledge and be obedient to Him by practising the teachings of Islam. A seeker cannot progress without both knowledge and obedience. Knowledge without obedience is of no benefit at all.

Ghawth al-Aʿẓam Shaykh ʿAbd al-Qādir al-Jīlānī has stated: "O claimant of knowledge! Your knowledge without practising it is not reliable and your practice is not credible without sincerity, because it is a body without a soul. The sign of sincerity is that you do not pay attention to the praise of people and the services rendered by them to you." [101]

Alongside having knowledge and practising it, it is also absolutely necessary to have the correct creed. Without sound creed, practice is

---

99 Ibn ʿAjība, *Īqāẓ al-Himam fī Sharḥ al-Ḥikam*, p.18.

100 Qur'ān 61:3.

101 ʿAbd al-Qādir al-Jīlānī, *al-Fatḥ al-Rabbānī*, p.148.

not acceptable. The method of correcting creed is to follow the creed and beliefs of the Companions, the Successors and the pious predecessors. This is also the teaching of the Holy Qur'ān:

﴿ٱهْدِنَا ٱلصِّرَٰطَ ٱلْمُسْتَقِيمَ ۝٥ صِرَٰطَ ٱلَّذِينَ أَنْعَمْتَ عَلَيْهِمْ﴾

Show us the straight path, the path of those upon whom You have bestowed Your favours.[102]

The straight path (*al-ṣirāṭ al-mustaqīm*) is the way of the Ahl al-Sunna wa al-Jamāʿa, which is also in accordance with the saying of the Holy Prophet ﷺ:

مَا أَنَا عَلَيْهِ وَأَصْحَابِي.

It is the path which I and my Companions are on.[103]

This path is the path of the Companions, the Prophet's venerable family (Ahl al-Bayt), the Successors, the Imams, the hadith scholars and saints (*awliyā'*) – and this is the true path.

It is essential that the seeker (*sālik*) has a firm footing in creed but should categorically refrain from matters of doctrinal disputes and polemical discourse. These creedal issues are not beneficial for the seeker. In addition to this, the beginner should avoid intricate issues of Divine Oneness (*tawḥīd*), such as discussions on the Unity of Existence (*waḥda al-wujūd*), Unity of Perception (*waḥda al-shuhūd*) and Descent through Five Presences (*tanazzulāt al-khamsa*). There is no benefit in these discussions and they can cause harm. These matters are such that talking about them without spiritual realisation and witnessing leads to more harm than good.

The primary obligation upon the novice seeker after acquiring knowledge of the Sharia is to be obedient to God in all aspects of life, outwardly and inwardly, day and night, and in private and public. Following of the Sunna should be the dominant factor in all worship

---

102 Qur'ān 1:5-6.

103 Narrated by al-Tirmidhī in *al-Sunan*: *Abwāb al-Īmān* [The Chapters on Faith], chapter: 'On the splitting of this *Umma*', 4:323 §2641.

and worldly matters. The novice seeker should only be connected to righteousness and become detached from every sin, and if a sin is committed due to forgetfulness, then immediate repentance should be sought in the court of Allah ﷻ. There should be complete certitude that forgiveness will be granted because the Holy Prophet ﷺ stated regarding the one who repents:

اَلتَّائِبُ مِنَ الذَّنْبِ كَمَنْ لَا ذَنْبَ لَهُ.

> The one who repents from a sin is like the one who has never sinned.[104]

To obey Almighty Allah ﷻ, it is necessary to adhere to the obligatory and compulsory actions and to adopt the Sunna. Along with that, the following routine is also recommended for the seeker (*sālik*):

1. Praying the daily supererogatory prayers (*nawāfil*)
2. Recitation of the Holy Qur'ān
3. Abundance of salutations upon the Holy Prophet ﷺ (*ṣalāt ʿalā al-Nabī* ﷺ)
4. Abundance of repentance (*istighfār*)
5. Giving charity (*ṣadaqa*)

In terms of seeking knowledge, it is important to sit in the company of pious scholars and to recite or listen to the Holy Qur'ān along with its translation daily. Likewise, the seeker should read or listen to some hadiths daily. There should be a regular routine of studying the Prophetic biography (*sīra*). In addition to that, simple books on Sufism (*taṣawwuf*) along with accounts of the saints (*awliyāʾ*) should be studied. There should be a rigorous study of jurisprudence (*fiqh*), and one of the four jurisprudential schools of thought (*madhhab*) should be adopted.

3.2 Following a Spiritual Master (Shaykh)

True adherence to the Qur'ān and Sunna is not possible without taking the means of a living guide. The technical term for this living guide is '*Shaykh*' (i.e. the spiritual master). Other terms for a spiritual guide are

[104] Narrated by Ibn Mājah in *al-Sunan*: *Kitāb al-Zuhd* [The Book of Abstinence], chapter: 'Repentance', 2:1419 §4250.

'pīr' and *'murshid'*.

3.2.1 The Need for a Living Guide

The Holy Qur'ān is not the word of the Holy Prophet ﷺ; it is the word of Allah ﷻ. However, it did not reach human beings directly. Had it been the case, all believers and disbelievers would have received revelation from the heavens and people would have received direct guidance. Instead, Allah ﷻ, in His infinite wisdom, created living guides among humanity who would be the intermediary to convey Allah's message to people. In line with this divine practice, a final intermediary was raised among humanity who had lived among the people for forty years – and he was none other than the Holy Prophet Muhammad ﷺ. Thus, guidance was provided to the people through his means.

Giving guidance through a living guide is the divine practice, and the same practice was adopted by the Holy Prophet ﷺ. The Holy Prophet Muhammad ﷺ did not send handwritten manuscripts of the Holy Qur'ān and hadith to other countries so that people could directly acquire the teachings of Islam. Rather, he ﷺ prepared a cohort of students and disciples, who were living examples of his teachings and who were illuminated with the divine light of guidance. The Holy Prophet ﷺ sent these guiding lights to different nations and tribes to convey to them the teachings of the Holy Qur'ān and his Sunna.

The Companions, Successors and the Followers were students, seekers and disciples. They possessed a greater capability of understanding the Holy Qur'ān and the hadith than the scholars of today, yet they were still in need of living guides. There is no science, discipline or craft that does not require a teacher or mentor. If such is the case with the material sciences, then for the spiritual sciences (i.e. *taṣawwuf*), which is much more obscure and abstruse than the other sciences, a teacher is most certainly needed. The journey of spiritual wayfaring requires guidance at every stage and so the process of purifying the lower self and attaining the gnosis of Allah ﷻ requires the direct mentorship of a living guide and *shaykh*.

3.2.2 THE MEANS OF ATTAINING SPIRITUAL EXCELLENCE (IḤSĀN)

The essential teachings of Islam can be self-taught. The apparent aspects of *īmān* and *islām* may be ascertained through books, however, matters of the heart such as the purification of the soul (*tazkiya al-nafs*), attaining the state of *iḥsān* (spiritual excellence) and correcting one's character is not possible without a perfected living guide (*murshid kāmil*).

The laws, regulations and principles that were required to be in written form were included into the books of hadith and *fiqh*. However, the things related to mystical experience and various types of spiritual states cannot be explained in writing but can only be understood by being in the company of someone who has mastered all the stages of the spiritual path (*sulūk*). Casting a reflection from one's heart to another heart can only be carried out by a perfected *shaykh*.

A perfected *shaykh* is not self-made through self-study. Just as the text of the Holy Qur'ān is accepted as the Word of God due to its continuous unbroken chains of transmission, and the hadiths such as those in *Ṣaḥīḥ al-Bukhārī* and *Ṣaḥīḥ Muslim* are accepted to be the words of the Holy Prophet Muhammad ﷺ only because they have been narrated through continuous reliable chains of narrators, likewise, the heart of the perfected *shaykh* is connected to the heart of the Holy Prophet Muhammad ﷺ through an unbroken chain of spiritual masters and disciples. A perfected *shaykh's* spiritual line is connected through such a chain to the fountainhead of all spirituality, purity and moral excellence – the Holy Prophet Muhammad ﷺ.

Just as Imam al-Bukhārī and Imam Muslim arranged the Prophetic traditions and the reports of the Companions in a codified manner in their voluminous compilations, in the same way, Imam Ḥasan al-Baṣrī and Imam Junayd al-Baghdādī used to enlighten their own hearts with spiritual secrets from the Holy Prophet ﷺ and the spiritual light of the Companions. In the case of the hadith scholars, the sayings of the Holy Prophet ﷺ were being copied from one book to the other, while in the case of the Sufis, the spiritual state of the Holy Prophet ﷺ was being transferred from one heart to the next.

Many Companions possessed a comprehensive grasp over both disciplines (i.e. hadith and *taṣawwuf*). Examples of such Companions are: Abū Bakr al-Ṣiddīq, ʿUmar b. al-Khaṭṭāb, ʿUthmān b. ʿAffān, ʿAlī b. Abī Ṭālib, Abū Dharr, Salmān al-Fārisī, Abū ʿUbayda, Abū Dardāʾ, Abū Hurayra, Muʿādh b. Jabal, ʿImrān b. Ḥusayn, Abū Mūsā al-Ashʿarī and others – Allah ﷻ be pleased with them all. These Companions became the mainstay for the practice of Sufism, and this is why the Sufis primarily relate their accounts and adopt their example.

The actual secret behind being a seeker (*sālik*) is the company of a perfected *shaykh*. The Arabic word for a Companion of the Holy Prophet ﷺ is *ṣaḥābī*, which shows the importance of 'companionship' (*ṣuḥba*). In Sufi terminology, becoming a seeker (*sālik*) of a perfected *shaykh* with whom the heart is inclined towards involves having presence of heart with the *shaykh* with complete humility and obedience. Doing so is compliance with the divine command, as stated in the Holy Qur'ān:

﴿يَـٰٓأَيُّهَا ٱلَّذِينَ ءَامَنُوا۟ ٱتَّقُوا۟ ٱللَّهَ وَكُونُوا۟ مَعَ ٱلصَّـٰدِقِينَ﴾

O believers! Fear Allah persistently and remain in the company of those who uphold the truth.[105]

This verse makes it clear that having faith and then practising is not enough, because after the command to adopt vigilance to God (*taqwā*), there is another distinct command: *'remain in the company of those who uphold the truth'*. So, the words *'O Believers'* refers to the completion of faith (*īmān*), which is the first grade; *'Fear Allah persistently'* refers to the completion of *islām*, which is the second grade; and *'and remain in the company of those who uphold the truth'* refers to spiritual excellence (*iḥsān*), which is the third grade. These were the three grades which the Holy Prophet ﷺ taught to the Companions in the Hadith Jibrīl. In this hadith, faith (*īmān*) is one's creed; *islām* is one's practice; and the higher grade of spiritual excellence (*iḥsān*) is one's inner state of witnessing.

Nawāb Ṣiddīq Ḥasan Khān Bopālī, who is followed by those who reject *taṣawwuf*, writes:

An Imam is one who has been declared to be an Imam by the

[105] Qur'ān 9:119.

> saints (*awliyā᾽*) and the guides of *ṭarīqa* (the Sufi path). This is the most supreme and best type because it is according to both the outward Sharia and the inward *ṭarīqa*. It is said that the perfection and dignity of humanity is dependent upon three things: the first is the purification of the outer; the second is the purification of the inner; and the third is emptying the heart. I say: the first is Islam; the second is *īmān*; and the third is *iḥsān*, which are all explained in the Hadith Jibrīl.[106]

Ḥājī Imdād Allāh Muhājir Makkī derives the importance of the *shaykh* from the previous and following verse:

﴿وَٱتَّبِعْ سَبِيلَ مَنْ أَنَابَ إِلَيَّ﴾

Follow someone who adopts the path of turning to Me.[107]

He also mentions the following statement in this regard:

الشَّيْخُ فِي قَوْمِهِ كَالنَّبِيِّ فِي أُمَّتِهِ.

> The spiritual guide (*shaykh*) among his people is like a Prophet in his community.[108]

He states further in relation to this:

> Whoever wants to sit with Allah ﷻ should sit with and adopt the company of the people of *taṣawwuf*. Just as the company of the Holy Prophet ﷺ was necessary for the Companions, likewise, the company of the *shaykh* is also necessary. If one is under the watchful eye of the perfected *shaykh* and obeys the *shaykh* to the letter, and he also places all of his discretion and intentions into the hands of the *shaykh*, then it is strongly hoped that he will reach the required destination.[109]

---

106 Nawāb Ṣiddīq Ḥasan Khān Bopālī, *al-Rawḍ al-Khaṣīb*, p.104.

107 Qur'ān 31:15.

108 Al-Ghazālī, *Iḥyā᾽ ʿUlūm al-Dīn*, 1:83.

109 Ḥājī Imdād Allāh, *Taṣfiya al-Qulūb*, p.4.

Shāh ʿAbd al-ʿAzīz Dihlawī writes:

> There should be a stern conviction that these aforementioned qualities depend upon the discretion of the *shaykh*, that he reforms and corrects people according to their individual conditions and states. It is stated in the Holy Qur'ān, 'So ask the people of *dhikr* if you yourself do not know'.[110]

Mawlānā Rashīd Aḥmad Gangohī writes on the need of having a spiritual guide (*shaykh*):

> The company of a perfected *shaykh* is vital for a seeker. Allah ﷻ states: *'O believers! Adopt vigilance to God* (taqwā) *and seek an intermediary* (wasīla) *to Allah.'*[111] In the *Iḥyāʾ ʿUlūm al-Dīn*, Imam al-Ghazālī has related a narration that the Holy Prophet ﷺ said: 'The spiritual guide (*shaykh*) among his people is like a Prophet in his community.'[112]

The very first condition given in verse 5:35 is faith (*īmān*) because the addressees are believers. The second is vigilance to God (*taqwā*) and this encompasses the whole of Islam. *Taqwā* is incomplete without obedience to the commandments and prohibitions, and the performance of other pious deeds. After this, the third phase is searching for a means (*wasīla*). The purpose of a *wasīla* is for man to reach the status of union with God through it. According to the learned scholars, the *wasīla* that is being referred to in this verse is none other than that of a perfected *shaykh*. Then under the supervision of the *shaykh*, the next stage mentioned in the verse is striving upon His path (*jihād*). The *jihād* referred to here is *jihād* against the lower self (*nafs*) which has been termed as the greatest *jihād* (*al-jihād al-akbar*).

Shāh Walī Allāh Dihlawī explains the meaning of *wasīla* mentioned in this verse:

> Sainthood (*al-wilāya al-kubrā*) has six requirements. Four of them are those mentioned in the Holy Qur'ān in the same order. The first is faith (*īmān*) i.e. proclamation by the

---

110 Shāh ʿAbd al-ʿAzīz, *Tafsīr ʿAzīzī*, 29:233.

111 Qur'ān 5:35.

112 Rashīd Aḥmad Gangohī, *Imdād al-Sulūk*, p.20.

> tongue and affirmation by the heart. The second is *taqwā* which is to abide by the commandments and refrain from the prohibitions. The third is to look for a spiritual *shaykh*; this is what is meant by *wasīla*. Union (the required destination) can only be gained through the *shaykh*, as it is the *shaykh* who shows the way. The fourth is *jihād*, which is to obliterate the lower self (*nafs*) and the ego.[113]

Shāh Ismāʿīl Dihlawī writes in the exegesis to this verse 5:35:

> For true salvation, before beginning inner struggle (*mujāhada*), it is necessary to find a spiritual guide (*shaykh*) and Allah's *Sunna* is also on this pattern because without a guide it is rare to acquire the desired path.[114]

Shaykh ʿAbd al-Qādir al-Jīlānī writes in *Ghunya al-Ṭālibīn* in the chapter on the etiquettes of a seeker with the *Shaykh*:

> وَلِيَتَحَقَّق بِأَنَّ الله عَزَّ وَجَلَّ أَجْرَى الْعَادَةَ بِأَنْ يَكُونَ فِي الْأَرْضِ شَيْخٌ وَمُرِيدٌ صَاحِبٌ وَمَصْحُوبٌ، تَابِعٌ وَمَتْبُوعٌ مِنْ لَدُنْ آدَمَ إِلَى أَنْ تَقُومَ السَّاعَةُ.

> A seeker should be certain about the fact that Allah ﷻ has a preferred routine, from Prophet Ādam ﵇ till the Day of Judgement, that in this world there is a *shaykh* and a seeker, that there is a master and the disciple, and that there is a follower and the followed.[115]

Shāh Walī Allāh Dihlawī's statement on the need for a *Shaykh* is categorical upon the subject:

> أَنَّ التَّوَالُدَ وَالتَّنَاسُلَ الصُّورِيَّ لَا يَحْصُلُ بِغَيْرِ الْوَالِدِ وَالْوَالِدَةِ كَذَالِكَ التَّوَالُدُ الْمَعْنَوِيُّ حُصُولُهُ بِغَيْرِ الْمُرْشِدِ مُتَعَذَّرٌ قَالَ فِي

113 Shāh Walī Allāh Dihlawī, *Anfās al-ʿĀrifīn*, p.148.

114 Shāh Ismāʿīl Dihlawī, *Ṣirāṭ Mustaqīm*, p.101.

115 ʿAbd al-Qādir al-Jīlānī, *Ghunya al-Ṭālibīn*, 2:280.

رِسَالَةِ الْمَكِّيَّةِ: مَنْ لَا شَيْخَ لَهُ فَالشَّيْطَانُ شَيْخُهُ.

> Just as it is not possible to beget offspring without parents, in the same way inner progression is not possible without a *Shaykh*. This is why it is written in *Risāla al-Makkiyya*: 'The one who has no *Shaykh*, then Shayṭān is his *shaykh*.[116]

Since the time of the pious predecessors till today, there has been a consensus among scholars that a seeker remains reliant upon the *Shaykh* until he or she has reached the station of union with God. The reason being that the *Shaykh* leads the seeker to this station. After arriving at this lofty station, from here on, God takes the responsibility to guide the seeker. Thus, the seeker of the *Shaykh* now becomes the seeker of God.

Shāh Walī Allāh Dihlawī writes:

اِعْتَقِدْ أَنَّ شَيْخَكَ هَذَا مُوصِلُكَ إِلَى مَوْلَانٍ وَلَا تَعَلَّقَ قَلْبَكَ بِسَوَاهُ.

> It is imperative to believe that your *Shaykh* will lead you to the union of the Almighty. (Until that union, the condition is that) you do not connect your heart to anyone else other than your *Shaykh*.[117]

In this way, when the seeker through the means of the *Shaykh* reaches the required destination, which is the union of God, the heart of the seeker becomes connected to God. Now the seeker no longer requires the connection with the *Shaykh*.

Ḥājī Imdād Allāh Muhājir Makkī states in this regard:

> Always connect your heart with your *Shaykh* with the firm belief that he is the means to God, whom Allah ﷻ has appointed for you to receive His blessings and to reach His presence through his means. Always remain an embodiment of obedience and love towards your *Shaykh* so that the gate of abundant blessings opens for you. Do not let any doubt or objection about your *Shaykh* enter your heart because this can

---

116 Shāh Walī Allāh Dihlawī, *al-Intibāh fī Salāsil Awliyā' Allāh*, p.33.

117 Ibid., p.58.

> become an obstacle upon the path to God.[118]

Shāh ʿAbd al-Ḥaqq Dihlawī states:

> بدانه که مدد خواستن از شیخ مدد خواستن از حضرت پیغمبر است که نائب وجانشین اوست واین اعتقاد را بجزم برخود بندد.
>
> Know that to ask your *Shaykh* for help is to ask the Holy Prophet ﷺ for help because he is the deputy and representative of the Holy Prophet ﷺ. Adopt this belief with complete conviction.[119]

On the same basis, the scholar of the Deobandi movement, Mawlānā Shabbīr Aḥmad ʿUthmānī, in his *Ḥāshiya al-Qurʾān* (*Tafsīr ʿUthmānī*), writes in the exegesis of the Qur'ānic verse: '*(O Allah!) You alone do we worship and to You alone do we look for help*':

> Adopting a saintly person as a means to the mercy of God and taking him as an apparent means to seeking help from Allah ﷻ, not believing him to be an independent [agent], is permitted. This form of seeking help (*istiʿāna*) is in reality seeking help from God Himself.[120]

Mawlānā Rashīd Aḥmad Gangohī writes:

> The seeker should be certain that the soul (*rūḥ*) of the *Shaykh* is not confined to one place. Wherever the seeker may be, near or far, even if the *Shaykh* is far away, the seeker is not distant from him spiritually. When this belief is firmly held by the seeker and the *Shaykh* is continually remembered and kept in mind then a spiritual connection will develop. The seeker will then always receive astonishing benefits from the *Shaykh*.[121]

---

118 Ḥājī Imdād Allāh, *Taṣfiya al-Qulūb*, p.96.

119 Shāh ʿAbd al-Ḥaqq Dihlawī, *Majmūʿāt al-Makātīb wa al-Rasāʾil*, p.350.

120 Shabbīr Aḥmad ʿUthmānī, *Ḥāshiya al-Qurʾān* (*Tafsīr ʿUthmānī*), 1:52.

121 Rashīd Aḥmad Gangohī, *Imdād al-Sulūk*, p.24.

According to the etiquettes and mannerisms of following a *Shaykh*, when in the company of one's *Shaykh*, litanies and additional worship should be kept to a minimum, and instead serving the *Shaykh* should be seen as a unique and precious opportunity. Talking should be kept to a minimum in the presence of the *Shaykh* without the voice being raised. A deep connection of love should be established with the face of the *Shaykh* such that its image is imprinted upon one's heart and mind.

When the seeker is apparently far away from the *Shaykh*, it should be contemplated that one is in his company. In seclusion, imagining the *Shaykh* creates an external as well as an internal connection with him. This ensures that spiritual blessings continue to be received from the *Shaykh*. A seeker can respect and have regard for other *Shuyūkh* but the heart must only be occupied with the love of one's *Shaykh*. It is essential that the seeker considers one's *Shaykh* to be at a higher grade than all other *Shuyūkh* alive upon the earth at that time. This must be held with conviction otherwise one would not be deserving of the spiritual blessings from the *Shaykh* because all of the seeker's love and attention is not directed at the *Shaykh*. This is known as Oneness of Quest (*tawḥīd al-maṭlab*).

In regard to this, Mawlānā Rashīd Aḥmad Gangohī writes:

> He must have a conviction that without this specific *Shaykh*, no one else can lead him to the required destination. If he does not use Oneness of Quest (*tawḥīd al-maṭlab*), then he will wonder around confused and depressed. In Oneness of Quest (*tawḥīd al-maṭlab*), the Shayṭān cannot appear in the form of one's *Shaykh*.[122]

It is necessary for the seeker (*sālik*) to supplicate to Allah ﷻ for a strong connection with the *Shaykh* and to desire the state of being annihilated in the *Shaykh* (*fanā' fī al-shaykh*).

Visualising the *Shaykh* and having love for him and a connection with him are more important for the seeker than all kinds of additional worship and spiritual struggle. It is necessary for the seeker to treat other disciples of the *Shaykh* well. One must pray for the good health and lofty ranks for the *Shaykh* and hold him dearer than anything else

[122] Ibid., p.22.

in the world. One should be submissive to the *Shaykh* in the way the dead body is in the hands of the one bathing it.

In this regard, Mawlāna Jalāl al-Dīn al-Rūmī writes:

No thing becomes a thing by itself
A piece of iron does not become a sword by itself
The *molvī* never became *mawlā-e-rūm*
Until he became the slave of Shams Tabrez

Fundamental Guidance for the Seeker: Three Steps in the Struggle Against the Lower Self

3.3 Limiting Food, Sleep and Speech – the First Step

The Messenger of Allah ﷺ has set out the path of salvation and forgiveness in his statement:

مَنْ صَمَتَ نَجَا.

Whoever maintains silence is saved.[123]

This is crucial advice for the seeker (*sālik*) that needs to be strictly adhered to. Speaking much will reduce spiritual experience and will take away the pleasures gained through spiritual endeavours. Mixing and interacting with people needs to be reduced. However, social responsibilities that are prescribed by Islam such as visiting the sick, seeing to those in need, fulfilling the rights of kinship, obtaining knowledge, earning a living, propagation of the religion etc. are to be fulfilled, but with only limited necessary speaking. Refraining from pointless and nonsensical talk and from laughing excessively is essential as these two habits cause the spiritual heart to die.

The tongue should only be in motion for the remembrance of Allah ﷻ and in preaching the teachings of Islam. After the *ʿIshāʾ* prayer it is

---

123 Narrated by al-Tirmidhī in *al-Sunan*: *Abwāb Ṣifa al-Qiyāma wa al-Raqāʾiq wa al-Warʿ* [The Chapters on the Description of the Day of Judgement, Heart Softening and Piety], Chapter: 'The hadith: "Whoever believes in Allah then let him honour his guest"', 4:660 §2501.

important for the seeker to avoid unnecessary talk; instead, he should maintain silence, and be in a reflective mood when going to bed. When the physical tongue remains silent, then the spiritual tongue of the heart opens and makes the seeker aware of Allah's gnosis and the hidden secrets.

With regards to eating, it is important for the seeker to not eat to his fill and neither to eat too little that it causes physical weakness. This helps the spiritual struggle to defeat the lower self (*nafs*) and to increase one's spiritual strength. In order to properly carry out worldly duties, the body should not become too weak. It is upon the individual to determine the suitable amount of food that is required to remain in balance in between the two extremes. Overeating enables the lower self (*nafs*) to overpower the individual, which results in becoming negligent. Whereas reduction in eating terminates the dominance of the lower self (*nafs*) and strengthens the soul (*rūḥ*). Doing so increases spirituality and inner light, and makes one subtle like the angels. It also creates a unique state of spiritual pleasure and satisfaction in one's worship.

فَالْخَيْرُ كُلُّ الْخَيْرِ فِي الْيَقَظَةِ؛ وَالشَّرُّ كُلُّ الشَّرِّ فِي النَّوْمِ وَالْغَفْلَةِ.

> All good is in staying awake and all evil is in sleep and negligence.[124]

It is necessary for the seeker to sleep less and to stay awake more. The 24-hour day should be divided into three parts: one for sleeping and two for staying awake. This leaves eight hours for sleep. It is better if that can be reduced further up to six hours, if possible. Then, if health permits, it should be reduced further.

It is advised to rest after lunch. Taking a siesta after lunch is beneficial. After the *ʿIshā'* prayer, it is better to stay awake and perform invocations (*adhkār*) and worship (*ʿibāda*). One should then go to bed without engaging in unnecessary worldly talk, to rise up again in the last part of the night to worship in seclusion so that He ﷻ may bestow His special benevolence upon His servant. If it is possible, then it is more beneficial to stay awake for half of the night. In the quiet of night, no one else will witness one's crying and humbling before the

124 ʿAbd al-Qādir al-Jīlānī, *Futūḥ al-Ghayb: Discourse no 94*, p.74.

Lord. Asking Allah ﷻ for His pleasure, and asking for His forgiveness, bounties and blessings in the middle of the night, is the true treasure.

3.4 Abundant Remembrance of Allah (Dhikr) and Worship (ʿIbāda) – the Second Step

Once the seeker (*sālik*) has gained knowledge and practises it, and once he becomes a disciple under the guidance of a true *Shaykh*, and once he has taken the first step towards inner struggle by limiting food, sleep and talking, then he can take the next step of starting the ritual invocations (*adhkār*) with the permission of his *Shaykh*.

It is more beneficial to be punctual in performing the invocations and additional worship. A time should be fixed to recite the Holy Qur'ān—this will enlighten the heart. With regards to supererogatory prayers (*nawāfil*), along with the five obligatory prayers (*farāʾiḍ*), there are four additional prayers:

1. The pre-dawn prayer (*tahajjud*), which has eight units.
2. The post-sunrise prayer (*ishrāq*), which has two units.
3. The mid-morning prayer (*ḍuḥā*), which has four units.
4. The oft-returning prayer (*awwābīn*), which is after the *maghrib* prayer and consists of six units.

If it is not possible to offer the *ḍuḥā* prayer on its time because of one's commitments, then it can be offered together with the *ishrāq* prayer.

Worldly talk must be avoided between the *fajr* and *ishrāq* prayers and also between the *maghrib* and *awwābīn* prayers. In addition to these supererogatory prayers, the glorification prayer (*salāḥ al-tasbīḥ*) should be offered at least once a week, preferably on Friday.

3.4.1 Visitation of Graves

It is beneficial for the seeker to regularly visit the graves of Muslims and the shrines of the saints (*awliyāʾ*). Visiting the general graves of Muslims reminds one of death and the Hereafter. Anas b. Mālik ؓ narrates that the Messenger of Allah ﷺ said:

$$\text{نَهَيْتُكُمْ عَنْ زِيَارَةِ الْقُبُورِ ثُمَّ بَدَا لِي أَنَّهَا تُرِقُّ الْقَلْبَ، وَتُدْمِعُ الْعَيْنَ، وَتُذَكِّرُ الْآخِرَةَ، فَزُورُوهَا، وَلَا تَقُولُوا هُجْرًا.}$$

I used to prohibit you from visiting the graves, then it occurred to me that it softens the heart, makes the eyes weep and reminds one of the hereafter. So, visit them and do not utter anything which is not suitable.[125]

According to Sayyidunā ʿAlī :

$$\text{نَهَى رَسُولُ اللهِ ﷺ عَنْ زِيَارَةِ الْقُبُورِ. ثُمَّ قَالَ: إِنِّي كُنْتُ نَهَيْتُكُمْ عَنْ زِيَارَةِ الْقُبُورِ فَزُورُوهَا، تُذَكِّرُكُمُ الْآخِرَةَ.}$$

The Messenger of Allah ﷺ prohibited the visitation of the graves. He ﷺ said: "I used to prohibit you from visiting the graves, so visit them for they remind you of the hereafter."[126]

Abū Saʿīd al-Khudrī narrates that the Messenger of Allah ﷺ said:

$$\text{إِنِّي نَهَيْتُكُمْ عَنْ زِيَارَةِ الْقُبُورِ، فَزُورُوهَا فَإِنَّ فِيهَا عِبْرَةً.}$$

I used to prohibit you from visiting the graves, so visit them, for in them is an admonition.[127]

Ibn Masʿūd narrates that the Messenger of Allah ﷺ said:

$$\text{كُنْتُ نَهَيْتُكُمْ عَنْ زِيَارَةِ الْقُبُورِ، فَزُورُوهَا، فَإِنَّهَا تُزَهِّدُ فِي الدُّنْيَا وَتُذَكِّرُ الْآخِرَةَ.}$$

---

[125] Narrated by Aḥmad b. Ḥanbal in *al-Musnad*, 3:237 §13,512; Abū Yaʿlā in *al-Musnad*, 6:373 §3707; al-Bayhaqī in *al-Sunan al-Kubrā*, 4:77 §6990 & *Shuʿab al-Īmān*, 7:15 §9289; and al-Haythamī in *Majmaʿ al-Zawāʾid*, 5:65.

[126] Narrated by Aḥmad b. Ḥanbal in *al-Musnad*, 1:145 §1235; Ibn Abī Shayba in *al-Muṣannaf*, 3:29 §11,806; and Abū Yaʿlā in *al-Musnad*, 1:240 §278.

[127] Narrated by Aḥmad b. Ḥanbal in *al-Musnad*, 3:38 §11,347; al-Ḥākim in *al-Mustadrak*, 1:530 §1386; and al-Bayhaqī in *al-Sunan al-Kubrā*, 4:77 §6988.

> I used to prohibit you from visiting the graves, so visit them, for they cause renunciation of the world and remind (you) of the hereafter.[128]

Visiting the shrines of the *awliyā'* enables divine attraction (*jadhb*) and longing (*shawq*). Shāh Walī Allāh Dihlawī writes:

> بارواح طیبه مشائخ متوجه شود و برائی ایشان فاتحه بخواند یابه زیارت قبر ایشان رود واز انجا انجذاب دریوزه کند.
>
> One should focus on the spirits of the great saintly scholars and recite *fātiḥa* for them; or one should visit their shrines and collect the blessings that are available there.[129]

This is all related to the *Uwaysiyya* affinity. In the *Uwaysiyya* spiritual order, according to Shāh Walī Allāh Dihlawī and other scholars, the following points are important:

> ازینجاست حفظ اعراس مشائخ ومواظبت زیارت قبور ایشان والتزام فاتحه خواندن وصدقه دادن برائی ایشان واعتنائی تمام کردن به تعظیم اثار واولاد مشبان ایشان.
>
> Of those matters which are very important: to celebrate the annual death anniversary of saints, visiting their shrines regularly, always reciting *fātiḥa* for them, giving charity (*ṣadaqa*) on their behalf and honouring their children and relics.[130]

The best time to visit graves and shrines is on Thursday after the

---

128 Narrated by Ibn Mājah in *al-Sunan*: *Kitāb al-Janā'iz* [The Book of the Funeral Prayer], chapter: 'What has been related concerning visiting graves', 1:501 §1571; al-Mundhirī in *al-Targhīb wa al-Tarhīb*, 4:189 §5375; and al-Mubārakpūrī in *Tuḥfa al-Aḥwadhī*, 4:136.

129 Shāh Walī Allāh Dihlawī, *Hamaʿāt*, p.34.

130 Ibid., p.58.

ʿaṣr prayer or on Friday after the *fajr* or *ishrāq* prayers. It is important to refrain from ostentation (*riyāʾ*) with regards to worship, however, for the novice, there is no need to delve into the finer details of ostentation.

3.4.2 The Etiquette of Performing Dhikr

It is beneficial to be punctual in performing one's invocations (*adhkār*). The seeker should specify certain times in the day or night when there is free time and the invocations can be performed in seclusion, if possible. When performing *dhikr*, the stomach should not be totally full, nor totally empty. Eating to one's fill is detrimental for the seeker, except for the pre-dawn meal (*suḥūr*), when fasting.

From the etiquettes of *dhikr*, those that are considered to be necessary conditions are: not having a full stomach, free time, seclusion in a room with the door closed and dimmed lighting, being in a clean place, wearing clean clothes, facing the *qibla*, sitting down in the sitting position as performed in the ritual prayer, (however, sitting crossed legged is also permitted,) and visualising one's *Shaykh*. Prior to performing the *dhikr*, supererogatory prayers, repentance (*istighfār*), salutations upon the Holy Prophet ﷺ (*ṣalāwāt*) and recitation of the Holy Qur'ān should be performed to purify the heart and mind. This ensures that the *dhikr* will be beneficial.

It is incumbent upon the seeker to remove the love for material wealth and status. In order to do this, it should be considered that the world and its possessions are temporary. There should be certainty upon this so that one's attention is kept away from the world, so much so that even if a thought of it does enter the mind while performing *dhikr*, it does not create hindrances. There should be such self-control that when the seeker claims to love and desire Allah ﷻ alone, the heart should affirm this and not negate it. If this is not the case, then the sweetness of faith (*īmān*) will never be gained from the invocations (*adhkār*) and litanies (*waẓāʾif*).

3.4.3 The Remembrance of Negation and Affirmation (Dhikr al-Nafī wa al-Ithbāt)

After fulfilling these prerequisites, the seeker (*sālik*) may perform the specified invocations (*adhkār*). Performing the *dhikr* of negation and affirmation is highly beneficial. It is important for the seeker to pay attention to the fact that with regards to performing *dhikr*, the focus should not be on gaining maximum reward (*thawāb*). Reward will be duly awarded by Allah ﷿. Discourses as to which is more rewarding—silent *dhikr* or aloud *dhikr*—are to be avoided. The sole aim of the novice is to illuminate the heart through the remembrance of Allah ﷿ and for it to have an impact upon the heart so that darkness is removed. For this, aloud *dhikr* is the most effective.

3.4.4 THE METHOD OF PERFORMING DHIKR

The method of performing *dhikr* is to utter the words '*lā ilāha illā Allāh*' continuously and with a loud voice. With the eyes closed, the '*lā*' is uttered with the head lowered whilst imagining that one is looking above the navel and below the heart, and then the head is moved to the right shoulder while stretching out the *lā*. With the head facing the right shoulder, '*ilāha*' is uttered. Then, while moving the head in the other direction making a sharp strike upon the heart, the words, '*illā Allāh*' are uttered intensely so that the strike is felt upon the heart. In this manner, the head moves from right to left.

The *dhikr* should begin in a low voice with the pitch gradually increasing. As the voice gets louder and the rhythm becomes faster, the head movement is also to increase in pace, so much so that the appearance should resemble that of a mad person. One should be lost in the *dhikr* and become intoxicated by it so that the heart can receive the light of the *dhikr*. Shaykh ʿAbd al-Qādir al-Jīlānī states:

يَكُونُ الذَّاكِرُ عَلَى وُضُوءٍ تَامٍ وَيَذْكُرُ بِضَرْبٍ شَدِيدٍ وَصَوْتٍ قَوِيٍّ
حَتَّى يَحْصُلَ أَنْوَارُ الذَّاكِرِ فِي بَوَاطِنِ الذَّاكِرِينَ وَتُصِيرَ قُلُوبُهُمْ
أَحْيَاءً بِهَذِهِ الْأَنْوَارِ حَيَاةً أَبَدِيَّةً.

A performer of *dhikr* should be in the perfect state of ritual ablution (*wuḍūʾ*). He should perform *dhikr* with a loud voice while striking intensely so that the light created by the *dhikr* impacts the hearts of the other people engaged in the *dhikr*.

So that their hearts are given eternal life due to this divine light.[131]

Shāh Walī Allāh Dihlawī has mentioned some important points with regards to the method of performing *dhikr*:

جمهور اهل طریقت متفق اند بر اداره راس بذکر، وتنزیل آن برقلب، ورعایت شد و مد، وسبب آن آنست که این کیفیت سبب آنگیختن محبت است وسد خطرات.

There is a consensus among the people of *ṭarīqa* upon the permissibility of turning the head during *dhikr*, upon the state that is revealed upon the heart and upon the need to stretch or shorten words while performing it. The reason for this is that this physical act and state are a means of kindling love and preventing spiritual danger.[132]

Thus, it is proven that turning the head from side to side during *dhikr*, striking upon the heart and stretching or shortening the pronunciations of *'lā ilāha illā Allāh'* are necessary. Shāh Walī Allāh Dihlawī states regarding the striking upon the heart:

والا الله رابه تمام قوت بردل ضرب کند.

During *dhikr*, when uttering *'illā Allāh'*, strike upon the heart with full force.[133]

He further states regarding the desired state of the person performing *dhikr*:

باید کر برهیت مرد متواجد که سردل خود رانتواند پوشید باشد واگر این حال بی تکلف بدست نیاید باید که ادعائی آن حال کند

131 ʿAbd al-Qādir al-Jīlānī, *Sirr al-Asrār*, p.83.

132 Shāh Walī Allāh Dihlawī, *Hamaʿāt*, p.28.

133 Ibid.

و بہر صفت خود رابان کیفیت دهد باید که بلند گفتن بقدر ظهور وجد باشد هر چند گرمی وجد بیشتر صوت بلند تر وتواتر وشدت ضرب زیاده تر.

The state of the person performing *dhikr* should preferably be that of a person who is in the state of ecstasy and has lost the power to keep the secrets of his heart hidden. If it is not easy to get into this state, then he should try to do so. This state must be achieved. It should be uttered very loudly so that a state of ecstasy is expressed. The more the ecstatic state increases, the louder and regular it should be uttered, with the intensity of the striking increasing.[134]

3.4.5 Four Types of Dhikr

For common seekers, there are four types of *dhikr*:

1. Remembrance of the Material Realm (*dhikr nāsūtī*) like *'lā ilāha illā Allāh'*.
2. Remembrance of the Angelic Realm (*dhikr malakūtī*) like *'illā Allāh'*.
3. Remembrance of the Realm of Divine Power (*dhikr jabarūtī*) like *'Allāh'*.
4. Remembrance of the Realm of Divinity (*dhikr lāhūtī*) like *'hū hū'*.

The highest rank of all of these is *dhikr nasūtī* as the Holy Prophet ﷺ preferred it more.

In the initial stage, when saying *'lā ilāha'*, love of everything besides Allah ﷻ is to be negated. When this is established strongly in the heart then the next step is to negate the existence of all things besides Him ﷻ. Nawāb Ṣiddīq Ḥasan Khān Bopālī writes regarding the *dhikr* of negation and affirmation:

وقت گفتن لاَ اِلٰهَ اِلاَّ اللهُ ذات خود وجمیع ما سوی الله رادر حکم

134 Ibid.

عدم پندارد و در وقت گفتن الا اله ذات مجرد بی کیف حضرت رب باری تعالی را اثبات نماید و تصور امام بر صفت تعظیم و محبت هر چه تمامتر وبرین ذکر همیشه مداومت نماید تا انکه حضور ذات بی کیف او سبحانه بغیر تکلف لازم و دائم گردد.

When saying *'lā ilāha illā Allāh'*, everything besides Allah ﷻ and yourself should be considered to be non-existent. When saying *'illā Allāh'*, the being of Allah, the One, without any condition, state and limit should be affirmed and imagined with the utmost love and respect. This *dhikr* should be continued regularly until the time comes when the being of Allah ﷻ is permanently before him without him having to strive for it.[135]

While performing *dhikr*, a seeker should aim to see the divine light of God with the eyes closed so that everything in the universe may be encompassed by the seeker and by the heart of the seeker. Nawāb Ṣiddīq Ḥasan Khān Bopālī writes in relation to the remembrance (*dhikr*) of the essential name of Allah (*ism dhāt*):

اسم ذات را که عبارت از کلمة الله ست با مدوشد بادل خود بگوید و ضرب سازد که اثر گرمی آن در دل پیدا گردد و در هر بارو هر مرتبه تصور کند که هیچکس غیر الله مقصود و محبوب و مطلوب و معبود نیست تا آنکه دل خود را از محبت ما سوی الله خالی بیند و وجودات عالم و عالمیان را معدوم و اند و ذکر و مذکور یکی گردد و ذاکر هستی خود را فانی در هستی مذکوره پندارد ------ اشارت ست بد ان وَقُلِ اللهِ ثُمَّ ذَرْهُمْ فِي خَوْضِهِمْ يَلْعَبُونَ.

[135] Nawāb Ṣiddīq Ḥasan Khān Bopālī, *al-Rawḍ al-Khaṣīb*, p.105.

> The essential name of God, which is the word *'Allāh'*, should be uttered so that it is emanating from the heart with emphasis and is correctly elongated so that it creates heat within the heart. Each time it is uttered, one should imagine that besides Allah ﷻ, there is nothing that is the ideal, the beloved, the desired and the worshipped. This should be continued until the heart is seen to be empty of the love of everything other than Allah ﷻ. The world and the things in it should be considered to be non-existent. Then the remembrance (*dhikr*) and the one remembered (*madhkūr*) become one. The performer of *dhikr* (i.e. the *dhākir*) should consider their being to be lost into the divine being of the remembered one (Allah ﷻ). This is indicated in the following Qur'ānic verse, *'Say: Allah (is the One who revealed divine books, sent Prophets, and then sent the Holy Qur'ān for your guidance). So leave them (upon their state) so that they waste time upon their senseless activities.'*[136]

As my *Shaykh* guided me, during the *dhikr* of *'lā ilāha illā Allāh'*, the novice is to pay particular attention to elongate the *'lā'* and to pronounce the doubled consonant in *'illā'* correctly. Then the *'lām'* is to be elongated in *'ilāha'* and the *'hā''* is to be kept short. The words *'lā ilāha'* is the negation, and it is to be said in the same breath, while the words *'illā Allāh'* is the affirmation, and it is to be uttered straight away (after making the negation). The *'hā''* at the end of *'Allāh'* is full of blessings, so it should be uttered loudly.

When an ecstatic state is gained through the *dhikr* of negation and affirmation, then the Angelic *dhikr* (*dhikr malakūtī*), *'illā Allāh'*, should be practised with the strikes upon the heart being raised to the highest intensity.

When the heart begins to perform *dhikr*, one should remain silent and listen to the heart. My *Shaykh* also directed me not to drink water for at least thirty minutes after performing *dhikr* lest it extinguishes the heat of the *dhikr*.

The seeker is to continue the practice of performing *dhikr* constantly,

---

[136] Ibid., p.106.

making the heart accustomed to it. After some time, the seeker should begin to see light during the *dhikr*. The seeker should recognise this light and safeguard that state, ensuring that one's state does not go below it.

If the seeker prefers to perform the remembrance in the Realm of Divine Power (*dhikr jabarūtī*) and the remembrance in the Realm of Divinity (*dhikr lāhūtī*), then both should be combined to perform the *dhikr* of *'Allāh Hū'*. This *dhikr* should be performed to give life to the spiritual heart.

There is also the option of performing the 'breathing *dhikr*' which is optional. The method of performing it is to say *'lā ilāha'* when inhaling, without speaking, and to say *'illā Allāh'* when exhaling, while striking the heart intensely at the same time. To perform the breathing *dhikr* with *'Allāh Hū'*, the method is to say *'Allāh'* when inhaling and *'Hū'* when exhaling, striking the heart at the same time. Striking upon the heart will enable the heart to start performing the *dhikr* on its own.

Continuing to perform *dhikr* using these methods will gradually develop spiritual satisfaction, and this state should be safeguarded. At this juncture, the seeker begins to receive nourishment in the form of light and this gives the heart happiness and contentment. Another major sign of having reached this point is that one prefers silence and detests talking. Then, while sitting in seclusion and contemplating upon the heart, a calm satisfaction will be felt inside which is indescribable. An example of this is the great taste of some food that one has tasted but cannot be described or put into words. For others to taste the same food and to know its indescribable taste, the method is to experience it themselves. In the same way, the spiritual satisfaction that is gained through *dhikr* is indescribable, which can only be gained through experience.

The seeker should not consider these experiences and states to be a great achievement, doing so can lead to arrogance which will result in one falling into the pits of lowliness; neither should these experiences be disclosed to others; rather they should be kept secret. Being content with these preliminary blessings will result in spiritual advancement coming to a halt. Instead, one's focus should be beyond them, and one should engage in contemplation and meditation.

Shāh Walī Allāh Dihlawī writes in regard to *dhikr* that it should be performed like the way lovers perform it, not considering it to be a mere litany:

> ذکر کند بطور اهل محبت و عشق نه بطور وظیفه چنانکه سابقا میکرد واسعد ناس بذکر کی است که صحیح المزاج و قوی العشق باشد. و آنکه متساهل و مختل المزاج است یا صفت عشق و محبت بروی مستولی نمی شود او را ازین راه چندین بهره نیست.
>
> *Dhikr* should be performed like the people of extreme love perform it, like it used to be performed; it should not be considered to be a mere litany. The most fortunate of those who perform *dhikr* is the one who has the correct temperament and is strong in extreme love. Anyone who is lazy, who has a bad temperament, or the signs of extreme love have not manifested upon their exterior, will not particularly benefit from this path.[137]

The remembrance of Allah (*dhikr*) and invocations (*adhkār*) should be performed under the supervision of the *Shaykh* with his permission. Apart from this, the daily litanies should also be taken from the *Shaykh*. In this way, one is constantly under his watchful eye. It should be a daily routine to seek forgiveness (*istighfār*) at least one hundred times, following the Sunna of the Messenger of Allah ﷺ. Salutations upon the Holy Prophet ﷺ (*ṣalāt ʿalā al-Nabī*) should be recited abundantly.

While performing the invocations and litanies, it should be a constant practice to visualise the presence of the *Shaykh* so that perfect connection is maintained with the *Shaykh* at all times. The seeker will see saints and Prophets in dreams. The *Shaykh* will certainly come to the seeker's dreams to provide guidance upon these matters. When performing abundant *dhikr*, oil must be applied to the head so that the brain remains moist. This is very important; if it is not adhered to,

---

137 Shāh Walī Allāh Dihlawī, *Hamaʿāt*, p.27.

then the brain can become dry which will create an imbalance in the brain. This may be seen by others as a sign of having mental issues, so this precautionary measure is to be strictly adhered to.

3.4.6 ESTABLISHING CIRCLES OF DHIKR

It is also beneficial for the seeker to take part in *dhikr* circles. The progress and advancement that is gained to one's spiritual states through *dhikr* circles is difficult to achieve in seclusion. As a beginner, it is possible that being in seclusion a lot may lead to one beginning to detest it. So, every Thursday, a *dhikr* circle should be arranged with friends and fellow seekers to perform *dhikr* aloud. The *dhikr* performed by others has a profound effect upon the heart. The *dhikr* of one another will affect each other's hearts.

Circles of *dhikr* are beloved to Allah ﷻ and His Messenger ﷺ. Abū Hurayra رضي الله عنه narrates that the Holy Prophet ﷺ said:

يَقُولُ اللهُ تَعَالَى: أَنَا عِنْدَ ظَنِّ عَبْدِي بِي، وَأَنَا مَعَهُ إِذَا ذَكَرَنِي، فَإِنْ ذَكَرَنِي فِي نَفْسِهِ ذَكَرْتُهُ فِي نَفْسِي، وَإِنْ ذَكَرَنِي فِي مَلَإٍ ذَكَرْتُهُ فِي مَلَإٍ خَيْرٍ مِنْهُمْ، وَإِنْ تَقَرَّبَ إِلَيَّ شِبْرًا تَقَرَّبْتُ إِلَيْهِ ذِرَاعًا، وَإِنْ تَقَرَّبَ إِلَيَّ ذِرَاعًا تَقَرَّبْتُ إِلَيْهِ بَاعًا وَإِنْ أَتَانِي يَمْشِي أَتَيْتُهُ هَرْوَلَةً.

Allah ﷻ says: "I am as My servant thinks I am. I am with him when he remembers Me. If he remembers Me to himself, I remember him to Myself. If he remembers Me in a gathering, I remember him in a gathering better than his. If he approaches Me by a span, I approach him by a cubit, and if he approaches Me by a cubit, I approach him by a measure of two hand's span. If he comes to Me walking, I come to him running."[138]

---

[138] Narrated by al-Bukhārī in *al-Ṣaḥīḥ*: *Kitāb al-Tawḥīd* [The Book of Divine Oneness], chapter: 'God warns you that you beware of Him', 6:2694 §6970; Muslim in *al-Ṣaḥīḥ*: *Kitāb al-Dhikr wa al-Duʿāʾ wa al-Tawba wa al-Istighfār* [The Book of Remembrance, Supplication, Repentance and Seeking Forgiveness], chapter: 'The encouragement of remembering Allah' ﷻ, 4:2061 §2675; al-Tirmidhī in *al-Sunan*: *Kitāb al-Zuhd* [The Book of Renunciation], chapter: 'Having a good opinion of Allah

Muʿādh b. Anas ﷺ narrates from his father that the Holy Prophet ﷺ said:

قَالَ اللهُ تَعَالَى: لَا يَذْكُرُنِي عَبْدِي فِي نَفْسِهِ إِلَّا ذَكَرْتُهُ فِي مَلَأٍ مِنْ مَلَائِكَتِي وَلَا يَذْكُرُنِي فِي مَلَأٍ إِلَّا ذَكَرْتُهُ فِي الرَّفِيقِ الْأَعْلَى.

Allah ﷻ says: "My servant does not remember Me to himself, except that I remember him in a gathering of angels. And he does not remember Me in a gathering except that I remember him in the highest company."[139]

Abū Hurayra and Abū Saʿīd al-Khudrī ﷺ both witnessed that the Holy Prophet ﷺ said:

لَا يَقْعُدُ قَوْمٌ يَذْكُرُونَ اللهَ إِلَّا حَفَّتْهُمُ الْمَلَائِكَةُ، وَغَشِيَتْهُمُ الرَّحْمَةُ، وَنَزَلَتْ عَلَيْهِمُ السَّكِينَةُ، وَذَكَرَهُمُ اللهُ فِيمَنْ عِنْدَهُ.

A people do not sit together to remember Allah ﷻ except that the angels encompass them, mercy envelopes them, serenity descends upon them, and Allah ﷻ mentions them to those who are in His Holy Presence.[140]

ﷻ', 5:581 §3603; al-Nasāʾī in *al-Sunan al-Kubrā*, 4:412 §7730; and Ibn Mājah in *al-Sunan*: *Kitāb al-Adab* [The Book of Etiquette], chapter: 'The merits of practice', 2:1255 §3822.

[139] Narrated by al-Ṭabarānī in *al-Muʿjam al-Kabīr*, 20:182 §391; al-Mundhirī in *al-Targhīb wa al-Tarhīb*, 2:252 §2287; and al-Haythamī in *Majmaʿ al-Zawāʾid*, 10:78.

[140] Narrated by Muslim in *al-Ṣaḥīḥ*: *Kitāb al-Dhikr wa al-Duʿāʾ wa al-Tawba wa al-Istighfār* [The Book of Remembrance, Supplication, Repentance and Seeking Forgiveness], chapter: 'The excellence of gathering together for the recitation of the Qurʾān and for remembrance', 4:2074 §2700; Aḥmad b. Ḥanbal in *al-Musnad*, 3:92 §11,893; al-Tirmidhī in *al-Sunan*: *Kitāb al-Daʿawāt* [The Book of Supplications], chapter: 'What has been related concerning a people sitting together and then remembering Allah ﷻ and the bounties upon them', 5:459 §3378; Ibn Mājah in *al-Sunan*: *Kitāb al-Adab* [The Book of Etiquette], chapter: 'The merits of remembering (Allah ﷻ)', 2:1245 §3791; Ibn Ḥibbān in *al-Ṣaḥīḥ*, 3:136 §855; Abū Yaʿlā in *al-Musnad*, 11:20 §6159; Ibn Abī Shayba in *al-Muṣannaf*, 6:60 §29,475; and al-Ṭabarānī in *al-Muʿjam al-Awsaṭ*, 2:137 §1500.

Abū Hurayra ﷺ also narrates that the Holy Prophet ﷺ said:

إِنَّ لِلهِ تَعَالَى مَلَائِكَةً سَيَّارَةً فُضُلًا يَلْتَمِسُونَ مَجَالِسَ الذِّكْرِ، يَجْتَمِعُونَ عِنْدَ الذِّكْرِ، فَإِذَا مَرُّوا بِمَجْلِسٍ عَلَا بَعْضُهُمْ عَلَى بَعْضٍ حَتَّى يَبْلُغُوا الْعَرْشَ.

There are some additional angels of Allah ﷻ who travel around the earth seeking the gatherings of remembrance (*al-dhikr*). They congregate at the time of the remembrance, and whenever they pass such gatherings, they ascend upon one another until they reach the *ʿArsh*.[141]

In another narration, Abū Hurayra ﷺ narrates:

إِنَّ لِلَّهِ تَبَارَكَ وَتَعَالَى مَلَائِكَةً سَيَّارَةً، فُضُلًا يَتَتَبَّعُونَ مَجَالِسَ الذِّكْرِ، فَإِذَا وَجَدُوا مَجْلِسًا فِيهِ ذِكْرٌ قَعَدُوا مَعَهُمْ، وَحَفَّ بَعْضُهُمْ بَعْضًا بِأَجْنِحَتِهِمْ، حَتَّى يَمْلَئُوا مَا بَيْنَهُمْ وَبَيْنَ السَّمَاءِ الدُّنْيَا، فَإِذَا تَفَرَّقُوا عَرَجُوا وَصَعِدُوا إِلَى السَّمَاءِ، قَالَ: فَيَسْأَلُهُمُ اللهُ عَزَّ وَجَلَّ، وَهُوَ أَعْلَمُ بِهِمْ: مِنْ أَيْنَ جِئْتُمْ؟ فَيَقُولُونَ: جِئْنَا مِنْ عِنْدِ عِبَادٍ لَكَ فِي الْأَرْضِ، يُسَبِّحُونَكَ وَيُكَبِّرُونَكَ وَيُهَلِّلُونَكَ وَيَحْمَدُونَكَ وَيَسْأَلُونَكَ، قَالَ: وَمَاذَا يَسْأَلُونِي؟ قَالُوا: يَسْأَلُونَكَ جَنَّتَكَ، قَالَ: وَهَلْ رَأَوْا جَنَّتِي؟ قَالُوا: لَا، أَيْ رَبِّ قَالَ: فَكَيْفَ لَوْ رَأَوْا جَنَّتِي؟ قَالُوا: وَيَسْتَجِيرُونَكَ، قَالَ: وَمِمَّ يَسْتَجِيرُونَنِي؟ قَالُوا: مِنْ نَارِكَ يَا رَبِّ، قَالَ: وَهَلْ رَأَوْا نَارِي؟ قَالُوا: لَا، قَالَ: فَكَيْفَ لَوْ رَأَوْا نَارِي؟

141 Narrated by Muslim in *al-Ṣaḥīḥ*: *Kitāb al-Dhikr wa al-Duʿāʾ wa al-Tawba wa al-Istighfār* [The Book of Remembrance, Supplication, Repentance and Seeking Forgiveness], chapter: 'The merits of the gatherings of remembrance', 4:2069 §2689; Aḥmad b. Ḥanbal in *al-Musnad*, 2:358 §8689; and al-Mundhirī in *al-Targhīb wa al-Tarhīb*, 4:244 §5523.

قَالُوا: وَيَسْتَغْفِرُونَكَ، قَالَ: فَيَقُولُ: قَدْ غَفَرْتُ لَهُمْ فَأَعْطَيْتُهُمْ مَا سَأَلُوا، وَأَجَرْتُهُمْ مِمَّا اسْتَجَارُوا، قَالَ: فَيَقُولُونَ: رَبِّ فِيهِمْ فُلَانٌ عَبْدٌ خَطَّاءٌ، إِنَّمَا مَرَّ فَجَلَسَ مَعَهُمْ، قَالَ: فَيَقُولُ: وَلَهُ غَفَرْتُ هُمُ الْقَوْمُ لَا يَشْقَى بِهِمْ جَلِيسُهُمْ.

Undoubtedly, there are angels of Allah ﷻ who go around the world in search of the circles of the remembrance of Allah (*dhikr*). When they find a *dhikr* circle, they sit with those who are performing *dhikr* and cover the whole gathering with their wings such that they fill all that is between the people and the sky. When the people leave the sitting, the angels ascend towards the heavens and Allah ﷻ asks them, even though He knows better about them, 'Where are you coming from?' They say, 'We have come from Your servants on the earth who were doing Your *dhikr* with the words '*subḥānAllāh*, *Allāhu akbar*, *lā ilāha illā Allāh* and *alḥamdu li'Llāh*', and then they were supplicating to You.' Allah ﷻ then asks, 'What are they asking me for?' They say, 'They were asking for Your Paradise (*janna*).' Allah ﷻ replies, 'Have they seen My Paradise?' They say, 'No, they have not, O Lord!' So Allah ﷻ says, 'Then how would their state be if they had seen My Paradise?' The angels say, 'They were seeking Your shelter from something.' Allah ﷻ says, 'What were they seeking My shelter from?' They say, 'From Your Hellfire O Lord!' Allah ﷻ says, 'Have they seen My Hellfire?' They say, 'No, they have not seen Your Hellfire.' Then Allah ﷻ says, 'Then how will their state be if they had seen it?' They then say, 'They were seeking Your forgiveness.' The Holy Prophet ﷺ said that Allah ﷻ says, 'I have forgiven them and granted them whatever they had asked for, and I have granted them shelter from that which they sought refuge.' Then the Holy Prophet ﷺ said: 'The angels then say: 'O Lord! Among them was so and so who was a sinful person, he was passing by and upon seeing them he just sat with them." The Holy Prophet ﷺ said: 'Allah ﷻ says,

'And he too is forgiven. They are such people that the one sitting in their company is not deprived.''[142]

In a similar narration from Abū Hurayra ﵁, the Messenger of Allah ﷺ said:

إِنَّ لِلّٰهِ مَلَائِكَةً يَطُوفُونَ فِي الطُّرُقِ، يَلْتَمِسُونَ أَهْلَ الذِّكْرِ، فَإِذَا وَجَدُوْا قَوْمًا يَذْكُرُونَ اللهَ تَنَادَوْا: هَلُمُّوا إِلَى حَاجَتِكُمْ، قَالَ: فَيَحُفُّونَهُمْ بِأَجْنِحَتِهِمْ إِلَى السَّمَاءِ الدُّنْيَا، قَالَ: فَيَسْأَلُهُمْ رَبُّهُمْ. وَهُوَ أَعْلَمُ مِنْهُمْ: مَا يَقُولُ عِبَادِي؟ قَالُوا: يَقُولُونَ: يُسَبِّحُونَكَ وَيُكَبِّرُونَكَ وَيَحْمَدُونَكَ وَيُمَجِّدُونَكَ قَالَ: فَيَقُولُ: هَلْ رَأَوْنِي؟ قَالَ: فَيَقُولُونَ. لَا، وَاللهِ، مَا رَأَوْكَ قَالَ: فَيَقُولُ: وَكَيْفَ لَوْ رَأَوْنِي؟ قَالَ: يَقُولُونَ: لَوْ رَأَوْكَ كَانُوا أَشَدَّ لَكَ عِبَادَةً وَأَشَدَّ لَكَ تَمْجِيدًا وَتَحْمِيدًا، وَأَكْثَرَ لَكَ تَسْبِيحًا.

قَالَ: فَيَقُولُ: فَمَا يَسْأَلُونِي؟ قَالَ: يَسْأَلُونَكَ الْجَنَّةَ، قَالَ: يَقُولُ: وَهَلْ رَأَوْهَا؟ قَالَ: يَقُولُونَ: لَا، وَاللهِ، يَا رَبِّ، مَا رَأَوْهَا، قَالَ: يَقُولُ: فَكَيْفَ لَوْ أَنَّهُمْ رَأَوْهَا؟ قَالَ: يَقُولُونَ: لَوْ أَنَّهُمْ رَأَوْهَا كَانُوا أَشَدَّ عَلَيْهَا حِرْصًا، وَأَشَدَّ لَهَا طَلَبًا وَأَعْظَمَ فِيهَا رَغْبَةً، قَالَ: فَمِمَّ يَتَعَوَّذُونَ؟ قَالَ: يَقُولُونَ: مِنَ النَّارِ، قَالَ: يَقُولُ: وَهَلْ رَأَوْهَا؟ قَالَ: يَقُولُونَ: لَا، وَاللهِ، يَا رَبِّ، مَا رَأَوْهَا، قَالَ: يَقُولُ: فَكَيْفَ لَوْ رَأَوْهَا؟ قَالَ: يَقُولُونَ: لَوْ رَأَوْهَا كَانُوا أَشَدَّ مِنْهَا فِرَارًا، وَأَشَدَّ لَهَا مَخَافَةً قَالَ: فَيَقُولُ: فَأُشْهِدُكُمْ أَنِّي قَدْ غَفَرْتُ لَهُمْ، قَالَ: يَقُولُ مَلَكٌ مِنَ

---

[142] Narrated by Muslim in *al-Ṣaḥīḥ*: *Kitāb al-Dhikr wa al-Duʿā wa al-Tawba wa al-Istighfār* [The Book of Allah's Remembrance, Supplications, Repentance and Seeking Forgiveness], chapter: 'The merits of the circles of Allah's Remembrance', 4:2069 §2689.

الْـمَلَائِكَةِ: فِيهِمْ فُلَانٌ، لَيْسَ مِنْهُمْ، إِنَّمَا جَاءَ لِـحَاجَةٍ، قَالَ: هُمُ الْـجُلَسَاءُ، لَا يَشْقَى بِهِمْ جَلِيسُهُمْ.

There are angels of Allah ﷻ who patrol the streets in search of the people of the remembrance of Allah (*dhikr*). When they find a people remembering Allah ﷻ, they call out, 'Come to your need.' Then they cover the whole gathering with their wings such that they fill all that is between the heavens and the earth. Allah ﷻ asks them, even though He knows better about them, 'What are My servants saying?' The angels reply, 'They are glorifying, extolling, praising and exalting You.' Allah ﷻ then asks, 'Have they seen Me?' They say, 'No, by Allah, they have not seen You.' Allah ﷻ replies, 'Then how would their state be if they had seen Me?' They replied, 'Had they seen You, they would have worshipped You more intensely and praised and exalted You more and would have increased in their glorification.' Allah ﷻ then asks, 'What are they seeking?' They reply, 'They are seeking Your Paradise.' Allah ﷻ then asks, 'Have they seen My Paradise?' They say, 'No, by Allah, Our Lord, they have not seen it.' So Allah ﷻ says, 'Then how would their state be if they had seen My Paradise?' The angels say, 'Had they seen it, they would want it ever more and be more intense in their desire for it and have greater inclination towards it.' Allah ﷻ says, 'What were they seeking My shelter from?' They say, 'From Your Hellfire.' Allah ﷻ says, 'Have they seen My Hellfire?' They say, 'No, by Allah, O our Lord, they have not seen Your Hellfire.' Then Allah ﷻ says, 'Then how will their state be if they had seen it?' They then said, 'They would want to flee from it even more and be more intense in their fear of it.' Then Allah ﷻ will say, 'I make you all witness that I have forgiven them.' Then the Holy Prophet ﷺ said: "One of the angels will then say: 'Among them was so and so, and he was not from among them. He only came for the fulfillment of his need.' Allah ﷻwill say, 'They are such people that the one sitting in their company is not deprived.'"[143]

3.5 Contemplation (Tafakkur) and Meditation (Murāqaba) – the Third Step

When the seeker (*sālik*) has gained the state of spiritual ecstasy and enjoys seclusion and silence, then mixing with and talking to people should be reduced. Speaking to people should be limited to the bare minimum, and most of one's time should be spent in seclusion. This is so that the state of ecstasy and longing takes root inside and becomes established in the heart. Upon reaching this stage on the spiritual path (*ṭarīqa*), contemplation (*tafakkur*) and meditation (*murāqaba*) should be started.

The meaning of contemplation (*tafakkur*) and meditation (*murāqaba*) is to utilise all of one's strength, intellect and perception in knowing the attributes of God. Another method is to imagine the terrifying scenes on the Day of Judgement or to focus upon the power of God in this universe, so that one is totally engrossed in pondering and contemplating to the extent that one's intellect, imagination and senses are totally in compliance. One should be overcome by such a spiritual state that the invisible becomes visible. Very fortunate is the one who has been naturally blessed with this ability.

Contemplation (*tafakkur*) and meditation (*murāqaba*) rely entirely upon perfect *tawajjuh* (spiritual concentration, focus and attention). When performing contemplation (*tafakkur*) and meditation (*murāqaba*) in seclusion one should imagine the light of God encompasses the whole universe. When focussing, it should be considered that the light of God is illuminating everything from the outside to the inside, from the top to the bottom, from the right to the left, and from all directions. Although the light of God is free from having any direction or corporeality, it should be imagined that the whole universe is functioning due to His light. The comprehensiveness of the divine

143 Narrated by al-Bukhārī in *al-Ṣaḥīḥ*: *Kitāb al-Daʿawāt* [The Book of Supplications], chapter: 'The excellence of remembering Allah' ﷻ, 5:2353 §6045; Ibn Ḥibbān in *al-Ṣaḥīḥ*, 3:139 §857; al-Bayhaqī in *Shuʿab al-Īmān*, 1:399 §531; Ibn Rajab al-Ḥanbalī in *Jāmiʿ al-ʿUlūm wa al-Ḥikam*, 1:345; and al-Mundhirī in *al-Targhīb wa al-Tarhīb*, 2:258 §2316.

being is to be imagined as to having such form that His light can be seen from every direction. It should also be firmly believed that this imagination of the manifestation of the divine light in the whole universe is not a result of one's inner struggle or meditation but that the light manifests itself.

Through this, the heart of the seeker will be illuminated, and the seeker will see rays of light emanating from it. The Holy Qur'ān states:

﴿فَأَيْنَمَا تُوَلُّوا۟ فَثَمَّ وَجْهُ ٱللَّهِ﴾

So whichever direction you turn to, there is the presence of Allah.[144]

Reaching this station is wholly dependent upon the ability of the seeker (*sālik*). After becoming firm and established upon this station, one can take the second step towards the next station, which is to imagine the light of God in the same way but to also deny the existence of all other things. The existence of all things that were encompassed by the divine light from all directions are imagined to be null and void. As a result, with the inexistence of all things, now the light of God will manifest itself being pure from any direction or position. In the first station, the divine light was seen in relation to other things but now it will be seen directly, without them. This is known as the 'colourless affinity'. This requires hard work and when the fruit of this hard work is achieved, one will be left amazed. Imagining the light of God, known as the 'witnessed light', is the first step in contemplation and meditation, and the stage of the 'colourless affinity' is the second step.

When this state has firmly taken hold inside then the *Shaykh* will direct the seeker to a specific affinity (*nisba*). The word *'tawajjuh'* (concentration, focus and attention) is used for this affinity. In order to direct the seeker towards the divine being, the *Shaykh* will prescribe the *dhikr* of a specific affinity and focus (*tawajjuh*). The reality of affinity (*nisba*) and its kinds will be discussed later in detail.

Among the Sufi Shaykhs, there are various types of meditation (*murāqaba*) that are prevalent. Some types of meditation are devised to prevent the heart from scattered thoughts and to totally focus upon the

---

144 Qur'ān 2:115.

Divine Being. In these types of meditation, an exercise of looking at the tip of the nose is conducted. Some types of meditation are devised to suppress the desires of the lower self (*nafs*) and to enable it to fully focus upon the Divine Being. An exercise of continually looking at the sun or focussing the eyes into outer space (sky) is carried out. Other types of meditation have the aim of enabling the lower self (*nafs*) to gradually build the ability inside it to give a form to imaginations. For this, an exercise of looking at the word *'Allāh'* written in Arabic upon a piece of paper is practised. In the same way, there are some other types of meditation in which methods are selected to focus attention (*tawajjuh*) upon God. This *tawajjuh* (attention, focus and concentration) is of two kinds: one is focusing upon the name and the second is focussing upon the one whom the name is attributed to.

When this state is achieved through meditation (*murāqaba*), then the seeker, according to the terminology of the inner subtleties (*laṭā'if*), has attained the station known as the 'opening'. This means that the heart, brain and other faculties receive the ability to speak. In this regard, it is the practice of some *Shaykhs* to direct the seeker to adhere to a specific affinity (*nisba*) during meditation, for instance to perform the *dhikr* of *'Anta fawqī anta taḥtī'* (You are above me; you are below me). This brings the path to the Affinity of Divine Oneness (*nisba al-tawḥīd*) closer. So this is a vast field in which different types of meditation have been adopted depending on the temperament and comprehension of the practitioners.

4

THE FOUR ESSENTIAL HUMAN CHARACTERISTICS ACCORDING TO THE SUFIS

Fundamentally, Sufism (*taṣawwuf*) is not exclusively about performing *dhikr* nor about specific rituals and appearances, however, these things are merely its branches. True Sufism (*taṣawwuf*) is to bring about a fundamental spiritual change that reforms one's morals and ethics, transforming one into an embodiment of excellent character. These characteristics and fundamental morals serve as the soil for the orchard of spirituality. These characteristics will be discussed in detail below.

Regarding the purification of the lower self (*nafs*), the purpose of Islam is to develop four characteristics in people. Anything that is contrary to or contradicts these four characteristics is to be negated. Allah ﷻ sent His Prophets to propagate these four characteristics and to encourage people to adopt them, with all the past divine laws sent down by God having the same purpose. Those rituals, deeds and actions that helped to develop these four characteristics were promoted. Thus, all the emphasis of the divine laws of the past was to create these four characteristics in people. Those things that contradict them have been warned against.

Righteousness (*birr*) comprises of those actions and means that develop these four characteristics. Those actions and means that negatively affect these characteristics are known as 'sin' (*ithm*).

The reality of perfect morals (*khuluq ḥasana*) is found in these four characteristics. Whoever has truly comprehended these four characteristics, and has understood the secret that the injunctions of every Sharia was the attainment of these four characteristics, is by all means a true jurist (*faqīh fī al-dīn*) and a truly knowledgeable person (*rāsikh fī al-ʿilm*). Whoever finds the clues to these characteristics in the outward practices of the Sharia, fully adopts them and absorbs the effects of these characteristics in his or her character, is one of the spiritually excellent people (*muḥsinīn*).

4.1 The First Characteristic: Purity (Ṭahāra)

The first of these four characteristics is purity (*ṭahāra*). Allah ﷻ has placed this characteristic inside every submissive and decent human being who has a natural inclination towards purity. If one remains in this natural state, with no external entity negatively interfering with the lower self (*nafs*), then this attribute of purity will be retained.

Purity (*ṭahāra*) here does not refer to the ritual ablution (*wuḍūʾ*) or the ritual bath (*ghusl*) etc. The meaning of purity (*ṭahāra*) here is the actual spirit of ablution and ritual bath etc. and the light and opening that is received from them. By having a bath, removing pubic hair, putting on clean or new clothes and wearing perfume, in this state one is attentive towards one's natural inclinations. Thus, one feels very happy and experiences inner tranquillity and an opening. However, when one is in the state of impurity, then the feeling is of darkness.

When the lower self (*nafs*) is surrounded by the darkness of impurity, then satanic whispers enter the heart. As a result, one has nightmares and darkness attacks the heart. When there is perpetual dominance of the light of purity (*ṭahāra*) upon the heart, then inspiration (*ilhām*) is received from the angels. Pleasant dreams are seen, and a light encompasses the heart both while awake and asleep.

The internal state created by the light of purity (*ṭahāra*) has the greatest resemblance with the Angelic Realm (*al-malaʾ al-aʿlā*) than other human states. The unique feature of this realm is that it is pure from all animalistic impurities. Those with the light of purity (*ṭahāra*) are a source of happiness and tranquillity for themselves.

4.2 THE SECOND CHARACTERISTIC: SUBMISSION AND HUMILITY (KHUSHŪᶜ WA KHUḌŪᶜ)

The second characteristic is submission and humility to Allah ﷻ (*khushūᶜ wa khuḍūᶜ*), which entails directing one's heart to Him ﷻ alone. When a person whose lower self (*nafs*) is sound and is free from inner needs and external worries – if during this state the attributes of Allah ﷻ and His majesty come to mind and the person's attention is directed towards Him, then this will result in a feeling of awe. As a result, an attribute of the sanctified realm that is beyond the material world enshrouds the person. When the person goes beyond the feeling of awe then the same awe takes the shape of submission and humility (*khushūᶜ wa khuḍūᶜ*). At this point, the state of the person is like a slave before his master, or a farmer before the king or a needy person before someone who is generous.

This state of submission and humility (*khushūᶜ wa khuḍūᶜ*) and supplicating in private (*munāja*) is similar to the state of the angels in the presence of Allah's majesty in the Angelic Realm (*al-malaʾ al-aᶜlā*). When the heart of a human being is fully immersed in the state of submission and humility (*khushūᶜ wa khuḍūᶜ*) and this trait becomes a part of one's essence, then a door is opened between the lower self (*nafs*) and the Angelic Realm. From this door, special knowledge and divine wisdom are received from the Angelic Realm, and they come in the form of illumination from Allah ﷻ that settles in the heart.

4.3 THE THIRD CHARACTERISTIC: RIGHTEOUS ATTRIBUTES (SAMĀḤA)

The third characteristic are righteous attributes (*samāḥa*). This means that a person is not a slave to the desires and lusts of the lower self (*nafs*) and does not engage in revenge, miserliness, greed etc. For the number of bad character traits there are inside a man, there are an equal number of opposite righteous character traits. So, there is a righteous category for every category of vice. For example, the character trait that controls carnal desires is abstinence and chastity (*ʿiffa*). Struggling and effort is there to counter laziness and negligence. Patience (*ṣabr*) is there to counter worry and depression. Clemency (*ʿafw*) is there to counter revenge. Contentment is there to counter greed. Being vigilant to the commands of Allah ﷻ (*taqwā*) is there to subdue the desire to transgress the boundaries set by the Sharia.

All of these things come under righteous attributes (*samāḥa*). The aim of all of them is to give total dominance to the pure commands given by the intellect over the animalistic desires of the lower self (*nafs*). The practices related to righteous attributes (*samāḥa*), mentioned above, should be practised continually so that its essence takes hold in oneself as an independent state. This state is then adopted by the lower self (*nafs*) as a permanent trait. This trait of *samāḥa* has also been named by the Sufis as asceticism (*zuhd*), spiritual freedom (*ḥurriya*) or abstinence from the world.

4.4 The Fourth Characteristic: Justice (ʿAdāla)

The final of the four characteristics is that of justice (*ʿadāla*). Justice (*ʿadāla*) is the bedrock of a fair and just legal and political system. It has many branches, one of which is moral conduct (*adab*). Moral conduct (*adab*) is a state that one adopts as a habit such that one constantly keeps a sharp eye over their actions and chooses the most suitable option. Another branch of justice is sufficiency (*kifāya*), which entails being prudent in all of one's affairs, such as in expenditure and business transactions. Maintaining ties is another branch of justice (*ʿadāla*), such as how one treats his or her friends, and one's ability to fulfil the needs of everyone around them, and in their general treatment of people. These attributes are various branches of justice (*ʿadāla*), all of which have only one purpose which is for the rational self (*nafs nāṭiqa*) to adopt a just system in accordance with its nature to be implemented.

When the characteristic of justice (*ʿadāla*) is found in someone in its most perfect form then that person becomes very similar to those in the Angelic Realm (*malaʾ al-aʿlā*) who are the source of God's blessings on earth. Then light is received from those people, like rays of sunlight. Conversely, anyone who opposes justice, or does not abide by the injunctions of the Sharia, or engages in conduct that harms people, then they are distanced from the people connected to the Angelic Realm (*malaʾ al-aʿlā*). Consequently, such people become embodiments of hatred and disorientation; they become disconnected from the blessed people, who are the means of recognising Allah's bounties and favours on the earth, and as a result, become plunged into darkness and are deprived of the connection to the Angelic Realm (*malaʾ al-aʿlā*).

4.5 ATTAINING THE FOUR CHARACTERISTICS AND THE STATE OF BENEVOLENCE (IḤSĀN)

To attain the attribute of purity (*ṭahāra*), practices such as the ritual ablution, ritual bath and others like them are obligated. To attain the attribute of submission and humility (*khushūʿ wa khuḍūʿ*), ritual prayers, supererogatory worship, supplication, recitation of the Holy Qur'ān, invocations, repentance and forgiveness etc. have been prescribed. To attain the attribute of righteousness (*samāḥa*), virtuous morals and manners such as forgiveness, philanthropy, charity, good manners etc. have been ordained. To attain the attribute of justice (*ʿadāla*), recommended acts such as visiting the sick, greeting people and adopting good etiquettes are specified.

After becoming acquainted with the inner state of benevolence (*iḥsān*) and having acquired it, if for some reason one finds that the state of benevolence (*iḥsān*) has not settled in their heart firmly or that it is not taking hold, then one needs to ascertain the reason behind it. For example: if the reason is one's disobedience and rebelliousness, then it can be addressed by fasting; if there is a domination of carnal desire, then it can be addressed by getting married; if it is because of meeting people a lot, then the cure is to sit in ritual seclusion (*iʿtikāf*) or to reduce the amount one mixes with others; if there are some random troubling thoughts settled in the mind, then the cure is to perform invocations and worship for a lengthened time; if the customs of one's locality have a negative impact upon one's state of benevolence (*iḥsān*), then the solution is to temporarily emigrate from the area or to remain in seclusion and increase the practice of contemplation and meditation (*murāqaba*). By addressing the preventative cause and by taking the steps required to remove it, one can facilitate the state of benevolence (*iḥsān*) to settle firmly in the heart.

5

THE SEVEN AFFINITIES

The best discourse on the seven affinities (*nisbāt*) has been provided by Shāh Walī Allāh Dihlawī. A summary of that discussion is presented here.

If a seeker (*sālik*) is able to create a positive internal state through spiritual practices and worship, such that the state entirely encompasses the soul (*rūḥ*), that state will remain settled in the person's interior and exterior and they will be completely dictated by it, so much so that they will continue to live in that state and die upon it. This spiritual state will become second nature to the seeker (*sālik*), and it never leaves the seeker (*sālik*). In this way, this state, which becomes firmly rooted inside the lower self (*nafs*), has now become an inherent and natural characteristic. The technical term for this spiritual state is 'affinity' (*nisba*).

5.1 The Affinity of Purity (Ṭahāra)

The first affinity (*nisba*) in the path of Sufism is purity (*ṭahāra*). The reality of this affinity is described as following:

After having a ritual bath and washing away any impurity, or after performing ablution and wearing clean clothes and putting on perfume, one feels a special kind of inner satisfaction and contentment. This feeling is not due to the physical but is an effect and reflection of the angelic power within the inner self. When one repeatedly experiences this feeling then the lower self (*nafs*) adopts it as a state which then becomes a permanent trait. Conversely, when one is impure or the body or clothes are dirty, then there is a feeling of narrowness and constraint. One's determination is no longer focussed and pure, and all kinds of worrying thoughts occupy the mind. However, as soon as one becomes pure again, one feels satisfaction and contentment inside and the earlier feeling of inner peace returns. When one realises that purity creates inner satisfaction and contentment, and impurity creates inner constriction and discomfort, then naturally one is inclined towards purity at all times. The state of ritual purity should be observed, and one is to always remain in that state.

When the seeker (*sālik*) internalises this state of purity, then a path opens up towards the Angelic realm. One witnesses an endless ocean of peace, calm and serenity. One then receives inspiration (*ilhām*) like the angels do. The angels are informed through inspiration (*ilhām*) to facilitate the betterment of that person according to God's will. After death, when arriving in the Hereafter, such a person is considered as one of the angels and then becomes one of them.

The sign of attaining the affinity of purity (*nisba al-ṭahāra*) and it settling in the heart is that angelic incidents take place upon the seeker such as seeing illuminated lights in front of oneself. The method of gaining the affinity of purity is for the seeker to go into seclusion then perform the ritual bath, put on new or washed clothes and then pray two units of supererogatory prayers. Then in order to dispel random thoughts and satanic whispers, the invocation '*yā nūru*' is to be recited abundantly. The ritual bath and ablution are to be performed repeatedly. The ritual prayer should be performed frequently, along with performing the remembrance of Allah (*dhikr*), then one should focus fully on whether one's state is similar to what it was before or if there is a change. If this is practised constantly, then the affinity of purity (*nisba al-ṭahāra*) will be gained. When it is gained it should be safeguarded and those things that disrupt this affinity should be avoided.

In this regard, it is important to realise that the reality of purity (*ṭahāra*) is not merely confined to the ritual ablution (*wuḍūʾ*) and the ritual bath (*ghusl*) but there are many other things that come under its purview. For example, the following matters are also included and are equally significant. They are:

- Keeping the beard, moustache and the hair tidy and well-groomed and not leaving it untended.
- Wearing pure and white clothes; and wearing perfume.
- Eating wholesome and nutritional food so that confusion and anxiety are avoided.
- Going to sleep in a state of purity and performing the remembrance of Allah (*dhikr*) before falling asleep; avoiding having random thoughts, removing toxins from the body and bringing comfort to the lower self (*nafs*) through fresh air and perfume.
- Giving charity; making good mention of the angels and saints (*awliyāʾ*); doing deeds that benefit people so that they are pleased and in return pray for you.
- Performing ritual seclusion at sacred places, mosques and shrines, or visiting the relics of the pious predecessors.

All of these things create a state of purity, or they strengthen it.

Adopting satanic behaviour and conduct, obscene talk, criticising saints and pious predecessors, doing something immoral, being in the company of beautiful women and adolescent males and continuing to think about their beauty, having thoughts about intercourse for a long time and engaging in more marital sexual intercourse than is naturally required, and keeping dogs and monkeys around oneself – all of these things are corruptive influences and negate the affinity of purity (*nisba al-ṭahāra*).

5.2 The Affinity of Obedience (Nisba al-Ṭāʿa)

The affinity of obedience (*nisba al-ṭāʿa*) is also known as the affinity of tranquillity (*nisba al-sakīna*). This affinity has three branches:

1. The sweetness of private prayer (*ḥalāwa al-munājāt*)
2. The encompassing mercy (*shumūl al-raḥma*)
3. The lights of divine names (*anwār al-asmāʾ al-ilāhiyya*)

5.2.1 The First Branch: The Sweetness of Private Prayer (Ḥalāwa al-Munājāt)

The reality of the sweetness of private prayer (*ḥalāwa al-munājāt*) with the Almighty is that when the seeker remembers Allah ﷻ during ritual prayer, invocations and supplications, one's attention no doubt turns towards the unseen reality of the words and actions. The person's rational self (*nafs nāṭiqa*) implicitly gains an overview of every unseen entity, and one derives pleasure from it. Thus, this 'attention towards the unseen' becomes a state of the lower self (*nafs*) and enters the essence of the soul. In this regard, it is common for someone to be completely silent but one's heart is full of this spiritual state. The 'attention of the seeker towards the unseen' is a general description. This is why it has been given other names like 'sweetness of private prayer (*munājāt*)', 'inclination towards *dhikr*', among others.

After attaining this general state of 'attention towards the unseen' the seeker naturally begins to perform an abundance of remembrance (*dhikr*), supplications and repentance. By fulfilling them willingly one's natural requirements are accomplished, and one can benefit from these practices with the help of one's insight and study. If these practices are not performed even for an instance, then the heart of the seeker feels anxious and feels like a lover who is separated from the beloved. However, once these practices are resumed then the earlier state returns together with its pleasure.

In order to gain this state, the Holy Prophet Muhammad ﷺ declared the following to be necessary: performing the remembrance of Allah (*dhikr*) in the morning and evening, reciting the supplications (*duʿā*), ritual bowing (*rukūʿ*) and ritual prostration (*sujūd*), making tearful supplications for one's wellbeing in the world and the Hereafter, seeking God's refuge from the evil of man and the Jinn and other similar practices.

The best method of acquiring this 'attention towards the unseen' is for the seeker (*sālik*) to keep the following hadith in mind. The Holy Prophet ﷺ said:

قَالَ اللهُ تَعَالَى: قَسَمْتُ الصَّلَاةَ بَيْنِي وَبَيْنَ عَبْدِي نِصْفَيْنِ وَلِعَبْدِي

مَا سَأَلَ فَإِذَا قَالَ الْعَبْدُ: ﴿ٱلْحَمْدُ لِلَّهِ رَبِّ ٱلْعَٰلَمِينَ﴾. قَالَ اللهُ تَعَالَى حَمِدَنِي عَبْدِي وَإِذَا قَالَ: ﴿ٱلرَّحْمَٰنِ ٱلرَّحِيمِ﴾. قَالَ اللهُ تَعَالَى أَثْنَى عَلَيَّ عَبْدِي . وَإِذَا قَالَ: ﴿مَٰلِكِ يَوْمِ ٱلدِّينِ﴾. قَالَ مَجَّدَنِي عَبْدِي - وَقَالَ مَرَّةً فَوَّضَ إِلَيَّ عَبْدِي - فَإِذَا قَالَ: ﴿إِيَّاكَ نَعْبُدُ وَإِيَّاكَ نَسْتَعِينُ﴾. قَالَ هَٰذَا بَيْنِي وَبَيْنَ عَبْدِي وَلِعَبْدِي مَا سَأَلَ . فَإِذَا قَالَ: ﴿ٱهْدِنَا ٱلصِّرَٰطَ ٱلْمُسْتَقِيمَ ۝٥ صِرَٰطَ ٱلَّذِينَ أَنْعَمْتَ عَلَيْهِمْ ۝٦ غَيْرِ ٱلْمَغْضُوبِ عَلَيْهِمْ وَلَا ٱلضَّآلِّينَ﴾. قَالَ هَٰذَا لِعَبْدِي وَلِعَبْدِي مَا سَأَلَ.

Allah the Exalted had said: "I have divided the prayer into two halves between Me and My servant, and My servant will receive what he asks." When the servant says: "All praise be to Allah alone, the Sustainer of all the worlds," Allah the Most High says: "My servant has praised Me." And when he (the servant) says: "Most Compassionate, Ever-Merciful," Allah the Most High says: "My servant has lauded Me." And when he (the servant) says: "Master of the Day of Judgment," He ﷻ says: "My servant has glorified Me," or sometimes He ﷻ would say: "My servant entrusted (his affairs) to Me." And when he (the worshipper) says: "You alone do we worship and to You alone do we look for help," He (Allah ﷻ) says: "This is between Me and My servant, and My servant will receive what he asks for." Then, when he (the worshipper) says: "Show us the straight path, the path of those upon whom You have bestowed Your favours, not of those who have been afflicted with wrath, nor of those who have gone astray," He (Allah ﷻ) says: "This is for My servant, and My servant will receive what he asks for."[145]

---

145 Narrated by Muslim in *al-Ṣaḥīḥ*: *Kitāb al-Salāt* [The Book of the Ritual Prayer], chapter: 'It is obligatory to recite *al-Fātiḥa* in every unit; if a person cannot recite *al-Fātiḥa* or cannot learn it, then he should recite whatever else he can manage', 1:296

Thus, to attain the 'attention towards the unseen', it is necessary to perform long prostrations in prayer, supplication and repentance by continually begging Allah ﷻ and to perform an abundance of the remembrance of Allah (*dhikr*), invocations and litanies.

5.2.2 The Second Branch: The Encompassing Mercy (Shumūl al-Raḥma)

It is important to know the reality of the affinity of encompassing mercy (*shumūl al-raḥma*). It has been witnessed repeatedly that blessings descend with the angels on the circles of Allah's remembrance (*ḥalaqa al-dhikr*), especially those that take place in the mosques. There is not an instant when people who engage in the remembrance of Allah (*dhikr*) and the ritual prayer do not receive such blessings. These blessings surround their lower self (*nafs*) like a fragrant breeze. This experience takes place irrespective of whether or not the group performing the remembrance of Allah (*dhikr*) are characterised by being in His divine presence.

It has also been repeatedly witnessed that when someone utters the word 'Allah' by emphasising upon the double *lām* and pronouncing it perfectly, then a ray of light imprints the form of this word onto the angels that are appointed upon the remembrance of Allah (*dhikr*). When *dhikr* is performed in abundance, the angels that are above these angels, receive this imprint. In this way the form of the glorious name continues to progress higher until it reaches the presence of Allah ﷻ known as the 'Precinct of the Sacred' (*ḥaẓīra al-quds*). Then the form receives a divine theophany (*tajallī*) which for the person commanding the higher position of the Greatest Individual (*al-shakhṣ al-akbar*)[146] is at the level of the spiritual heart (*qalb*).

It has also been witnessed on occasions that light surrounds the one who is performing the remembrance of Allah (*dhikr*) and the whole surrounding area is full of light. Allah ﷻ knows best about these matters.

---

§395.

[146] *Al-Shakhṣ al-akbar* is a term in the terminology of Gnosis (*maʿrifa*). It is a higher spiritual position and is a spiritual state of the soul (*rūḥ*). Ed.

In the same way, there are many kinds of obedience that sometimes do not have resemblance with the private supplication (*munajāt*) but are certainly the means of receiving blessings. For this reason, their performance is prescribed. This type of obedience include: sacrificing animals, performing circumambulation of the *Kaʿba*, running between Ṣafā and Marwa, viewing the *Kaʿba*, fasting, giving charity, struggling in the way of Allah ﷻ, visiting the sick, accompanying a funeral and other such good deeds.

With regards to gaining the affinity of comprehensive mercy (*shumūl al-raḥma*), as one continues to perform the invocations and required practices, the lower self (*nafs*) begins to gradually adopt the qualities of the affinity of comprehensive mercy, until it becomes a permanent state. The following hadith clarifies this. The Holy Prophet Muhammad ﷺ said that Allah ﷻ states:

وَمَا تَقَرَّبَ إِلَيَّ عَبْدِي بِشَيْءٍ أَحَبَّ إِلَيَّ مِمَّا افْتَرَضْتُ عَلَيْهِ، وَمَا يَزَالُ عَبْدِي يَتَقَرَّبُ إِلَيَّ بِالنَّوَافِلِ حَتَّى أُحِبَّهُ، فَإِذَا أَحْبَبْتُهُ كُنْتُ سَمْعَهُ الَّذِي يَسْمَعُ بِهِ، وَبَصَرَهُ الَّذِي يُبْصِرُ بِهِ، وَيَدَهُ الَّتِي يَبْطُشُ بِهَا وَرِجْلَهُ الَّتِي يَمْشِي بِهَا.

> And the most beloved things with which My slave comes nearer to Me, is what I have enjoined upon him; and My slave keeps on coming closer to Me through performing supererogatory prayers till I love him. And when I love him, I become his sense of hearing with which he hears, his sense of sight with which he sees, his hand with which he grips and his leg with which he walks.[147]

The attribute of comprehensive mercy (*shumūl al-raḥma*) is found predominantly in obligatory acts (*farāʾiḍ*), which is why the love of God is inclined towards them. When plenty of supererogatory prayers are performed then Allah ﷻ sends a light which, with the light of the

---

147 Narrated by al-Bukhārī in *al-Ṣaḥīḥ*: *Kitāb al-Riqāq* [The Book of Heart Softening Advice], chapter: 'The humility or modesty or lowliness', 8:105 §6502.

angels, enters the soul of the person and surrounds him so much so that the whole being of the soul depends upon it. That is, the divine light becomes sustenance for the soul. This light is the reason for supplications being accepted and the person being safeguarded from harm. This has been witnessed repeatedly.

The reality of the divine light being sustenance for the soul is best explained by the following verses of the Qur'ān:

﴿مَثَلُ نُورِهِۦ كَمِشْكَوٰةٍ فِيهَا مِصْبَاحٌ﴾

The example of Allah's light is such like a lamp in a niche.[148]

The Companion Ibn 'Abbās ؓ interpreted these words in the following manner:

مَثَلُ نُورِهِ فِي قَلْبِ الْمُؤْمِنِ.

The example of Allah's light in the heart of a believer (is such like a lamp in a niche).[149]

Meaning that when the light of Allah ﷻ enters the heart of a believer, it is like a lamp in a niche.

5.2.3 THE THIRD BRANCH: THE LIGHTS OF DIVINE NAMES (ANWĀR AL-ASMĀ' AL-ILĀHIYYA)

When the remembrance (*dhikr*) of the glorious names of Allah ﷻ is performed sincerely and with full attention and the heart is fully engaged in preserving the names within it, then the forms of the divine names unlock a door in the inner self from which light and coolness descend upon the heart. In this state, great pleasure is felt. When pleasure is felt by performing the remembrance (*dhikr*) of the divine names, then one engages in the *dhikr* with even more effort and attention; the more effort and attention that is put in, the more blessings are gained from the light. This is why it is emphasised that the words of the prescribed supplications should be pronounced

---

[148] Qur'ān 24:35.

[149] al-Rāzī, *al-Tafsīr al-Kabīr*, 23:203.

properly. Moreover, this is why some of the divine names of Allah ﷻ have been declared as the Greatest Name (*al-ism al-aʿẓam*) and some supplications have been associated to specific effects or results. Similarly, when a worshipper performs an abundance of ritual prayer, the remembrance of Allah (*dhikr*) and other acts of obedience, then the light of this obedience which has an independent form in the realm of forms establishes a connection with the worshipper, surrounding the lower self (*nafs*) and becoming its guardian.

The most assured way of gaining this affinity is through the remembrance (*dhikr*) of the essential name 'Allāh'. For this, one should empty their heart and mind of any random or disturbing thought and ensure they are not disturbed by anything such as needing to relieve themselves in the bathroom. One should also perform fresh ablution (*wuḍūʾ*) and then recite the essential name 'Allāh' one thousand times, followed by salutations upon the Holy Prophet ﷺ. While performing this *dhikr*, the double *lām* should be emphasised while pronouncing all the letters correctly. During this *dhikr*, that light which is spread in the atmosphere should be imagined intermittently.

When this *dhikr* is performed a few thousand times in this way, then a connection will be made with that light. After this, the state of the person will be such that when one intends to perform the praise and glorification of Allah ﷻ, repentance (*istighfār*) and other Qurʾānic invocations, then that light will adopt the colours of the attributes of these invocations and will become visible to the person. The effects of this light will appear inside the person as well as in the world around him.

The three branches mentioned above all come under the affinity of obedience (*nisba al-ṭāʿa*) and attaining them is the fruit of obedience. In some acts of obedience, one branch may predominate over the other two. In the lives of the Companions of the Holy Prophet ﷺ, their Successors and the Followers after them, the affinity of obedience (*nisba al-ṭāʿa*) was much more dominant and luminous. Their pious actions, worship and supplications reflected this affinity.

5.3 THE UWAYSIYYA AFFINITY (AL-NISBA AL-UWAYSIYYA)

From the affinities that are credible among the followers of *taṣawwuf* is the *Uwaysiyya* affinity (*al-Nisba al-Uwaysiyya*). It is considered to be an intermediary between the affinity of purity (*ṭahāra*) and the affinity of obedience (*ṭāʿa*), as it is connected to both.

The detailed explanation of the *Uwaysiyya* affinity is that the rational self (*nafs nāṭiqa*) is like a mirror which the spiritual states, as well as the physical states, reflect upon. There is a divinely instilled capacity in every spiritual and physical state. However, the capacities of the spiritual states and the physical states are opposite to one another. One of the spiritual states is that when the seeker of the spiritual path (*ṭarīqa*) comes out of the lowliness of the material world and he or she is in the heights of the Angelic Realm, rejecting all impurities, they are then absorbed in the pleasant and subtle states so much so that it is like their lower self (*nafs*) is lost inside these states. At this station, the condition of the seeker (*sālik*) is like a container that contains air and does not submerge when placed in the water.

When the lower self (*nafs*) attains this state, then the mirror of the heart receives a colour from above, due to the blessings of which a special congeniality is created with the souls of the righteous. Then the spiritual states of the pious soul, such as contentment, opening of the breast, divine attraction (*jadhb*), attention towards the realm of the unseen and disclosure of those realities that are secrets to others, are adopted. Whether the congeniality is created with the souls of the Prophets or the Saints, or with the angels is another question.

Sometimes, a seeker develops congeniality with a specific soul (*rūḥ*) because the seeker has learnt of the noble qualities of that pious person and thus developed great love for him. Due to this love, a vast path opens up between the seeker and the soul of this Saint. Another way is that the specific soul with which the seeker gained congeniality with was that of the seeker's *Shaykh* or from one of the seeker's pious predecessors. That soul (*rūḥ*) has the capacity of providing guidance to those who are attached to it. A third possible way is that congeniality is created with a specific soul due to the seeker's natural passion and requirement – this is something very difficult to understand. The seeker (*sālik*) sees this pious personality in dreams and benefits from him directly in the metaphysical realm.

5.3.1 Different Levels of Souls in the Metaphysical Realm

There are three different levels of souls in the metaphysical realm:

1. The supreme assembly (*al-mala᾽ al-aʿlā*)
2. The lower assembly (*al-mala᾽ al-sāfil*)
3. The souls of the *Shaykhs*

I. The Supreme Assembly (al-Mala᾽ al-Aʿlā)

When a seeker gains the *Uwaysiyya* affinity through the Supreme Assembly (*al-mala᾽ al-aʿlā*), then the unique features of this are that God's 'form of knowledge' is imprinted upon the tablet of the heart. This then makes apparent to the heart the four divine excellent qualities regarding the regulation of the universe, which are initiation (*ibdāʿ*), creation (*khalq*), management (*tadbīr*) and descension (*tadallī*). The seeker (*sālik*) gains the knowledge of these four divine qualities of God's power without any intention and without concentrating upon it. Sometimes, the plans and decisions regarding the system of the universe that are decided in the Holy Enclosure (*ḥaẓīra al-quds*) are imprinted upon the heart of the seeker due to the *Uwaysiyya* affinity.

II. The Lower Assembly (al-Mala᾽ al-Sāfil)

Below the Supreme Assembly is the Lower Assembly (*al-mala᾽ al-sāfil*). The sign of gaining the *Uwaysiyya* affinity through the Lower Assembly is that the seeker sees angels, both while awake and during dreams. The seeker (*sālik*) sees the angels in this level coming and going, doing the duties that are assigned to them and also recognises them.

III. The Souls of the Shaykhs

The third level of souls in the metaphysical realm is that of the *Shaykhs*. Whether the souls remained together or separately, it is necessary to develop love for these souls in order to gain the *Uwaysiyya* affinity through this level. The seeker (*sālik*) should develop the state of 'annihilation in the *Shaykh*' (*fanā᾽ fī al-shaykh*), which becomes effective in every aspect of the seeker's life, like the way water when it reaches the roots of a tree benefits every branch and leaf.

The affinity of 'annihilation in the *Shaykh*' (*fanāʾ fī al-shaykh*) does not have an equal effect on everyone, rather it is different for each person. With respect to this affinity, the necessary acts to perform for one's *Shaykh* include: arranging their annual death-anniversary (*ʿurs*), regularly visiting their grave and reciting *fātiḥa* for their soul, giving charity (*ṣadaqa*) on their behalf and fully respecting and honouring their relics, children and associates.

When having attained any of the above-mentioned affinities, the seeker will have a natural inclination towards the effects of that specific affinity. This happens regardless of whether or not one has any knowledge regarding that affinity or has seen anyone in that state. The reason being that the inclination towards this affinity is totally instinctual and natural.

When one of these affinities is gained, then whichever level of the metaphysical realm the affinity belongs to, the seeker sees the souls from that realm and takes benefit from their blessings. Whenever the seeker (*sālik*) faces danger or calamity, then those souls appear before him. In brief, other things similar to this that are received by the seeker are also the fruits of this affinity.

Possessing the *Uwaysiyya* affinity creates such a connection that it enters the essence of the soul of the seeker (*sālik*). This state is then experienced by the seeker whether awake or in a dream state. When asleep, the physical senses are free from the effect and control of the carnal desires and from bodily needs. In this condition, all those forms that are collected inside the heart, appear before the seeker in a dream and the seeker (*sālik*) focusses fully upon them. At this juncture, extraordinary things appear, and extraordinary affairs take shape.

Whichever affinity a seeker is connected to, the outcome of all of them is that many different kinds of incidents are seen in dreams and a lot of good news is received. Other people see the seeker (*sālik*) in their dreams, and due to the evidence of the individual's greatness that they see, they hold that person in high regard. Furthermore, the seeker (*sālik*) receives help from the unseen during times of hardship and calamities.

The first person to open the door of divine attraction (*jadhb*) and to set out on this path in the *Umma* of the Holy Prophet Muhammad ﷺ was the fourth Rightly Guided Caliph, ʿAlī ؓ. This is why all the spiritual orders (*ṭarīqas*) are associated to him. After him, there were the Saints (*awliyāʾ*) and the leaders of spiritual orders. From amongst them, the one who was the most exceptional, who was able to master the path of divine attraction (*jadhb*) and return to the essence of the *Uwaysiyya* affinity and progressed through it successfully, was Shaykh ʿAbd al-Qādir al-Jīlānī—Allah's mercy be upon him. It is because of this that it is said that he executes matters in the grave like the living do.

Furthermore, no one is more renowned in the *Umma* for performing miracles than these two holy personalities, i.e. the Rightly Guided Caliph ʿAlī ؓ and Shaykh ʿAbd al-Qādir al-Jīlānī. This fame of theirs requires that when the seeker (*sālik*) finds the attention of the realm of the unseen towards himself that he concentrates on one of these two personalities. In light of these points, nowadays, if a seeker gains congeniality with the soul of a specific *Shaykh* and attains blessings from him, then the actual reality will be that the blessings are most likely coming from either the connection with the Holy Prophet Muhammad ﷺ, or from the connection with Sayyidunā ʿAlī ؓ or from the connection with Shaykh ʿAbd al-Qādir al-Jīlānī.

5.4 The Affinity of Divine Gnosis (Nisba al-Maʿrifa)

From those affinities that are connected to the path of divine attraction (*jadhb*), one of them is the affinity of divine gnosis (*nisba al-maʿrifa*). Before understanding the affinity of divine gnosis, it should be understood that when knowledge of something is gained, it is as though the image of that thing that is imprinted on the mind is the true reality of that thing. An example of this is when looking at something while wearing glasses. When looking through the glasses and seeing something, at that time the role of the glasses does not come to mind, but it is as though the thing is being viewed directly. Another example is that of a tree upon the bank of a stream with its reflection being clearly visible in the water. A person, looking at the reflection, being engrossed in it so much that at that time it is not considered to be a reflection because the water no longer comes to the mind when viewing the reflection.

Now the question arises as to how man is able to gain knowledge about divine theophany or unveiling (*tajallī*). It is important to know that when divine theophany (*tajallī*) takes place in the shape of forms, and at that time human senses are free from the needs of the lower self (*nafs*), then the soul is totally focussed upon the form of the divine theophany (*tajallī*) which becomes a model of perfection for the soul. However, it is not necessary that the form of the divine theophany (*tajallī*) is witnessed only in a dream, sometimes it is also possible that when one is awake and the human senses are free from the needs of the lower self (*nafs*), then the form of the divine theophany (*tajallī*) can be seen while awake.

The question also arises as to why the divine theophany or unveiling (*tajallī*) appears in the shape of forms. In this regard, it is important to know that Allah ﷻ has granted humans two powers. One of them is the power of imagination (*takhayyul*), which is the power to provide form to those formless things before the eyes. With the help of the power of imagination (*takhayyul*), for example, anger is seen in the form of a wild animal and greed is seen in the form of a crow. The second is the power of clarity (*mutawahhima*). This takes forms and shapes and transfers them into meanings. An example of how this power works is remembering someone whom one has seen a long time ago. Then straight away there is a wish to recall the image of this person. The first thing that comes to mind is a general picture of this person. The picture is so general that it can be attributed to many other people. After this, the picture is gradually specified until the picture of the required person appears clearly in the mind. Another example of this is when a person who has memorised the whole Qur'ān has a general idea that a certain verse is in a particular chapter. The first thing that comes to mind is a general form of the verse, then gradually the form of the verse is specified to the required one.

In essence, the power of imagination (*mutakhayyila*) takes absolute or abstract meanings and transfers them into shapes and forms, while the power of clarity (*mutawahhima*) changes forms into abstract meanings. This preliminary discussion was required before discussing the affinity of gnosis (*nisba al-maʿrifa*).

When the seeker turns to the divine presence with full concentration of the heart and mind, all of the senses and feelings become completely subdued by the reality that the mind has perceived. Here, in the power of clarity (*mutawahhima*) of the Gnostic (*ʿārif*), a thought comes into being that gives a general indication of the reality that has no trace or sign. At this station, this thought does not have any specific shape or form, but it is purely an abstract reality. This abstract reality is in fact divine theophany (*tajallī*), which has descended upon the power of clarity (*mutawahhima*) of the Gnostic (*ʿārif*). In the same way, when this abstract reality is in the power of imagination (*mutakhayyila*) of the Gnostic (*ʿārif*), instead of the power of clarity (*mutawahhima*), the mind perceives a form. The Gnostic believes this to be divine theophany (*tajallī*). The difference between the two is that the first is known as the 'clarity' (*wahmī*) divine theophany (*tajallī*), and the second is known as the 'imagination' (*takhayyul*) divine theophany (*tajallī*).

When the Gnostic perceives the 'clarity' (*wahmī*) divine theophany (*tajallī*), then it must be safeguarded. As a result of guarding it and keeping a watchful eye, gradually a spacious path is opened towards the rank of 'no trace or sign'. This path develops great ability in the Gnostic, and it is this ability that is called the affinity of divine gnosis (*nisba al-maʿrifa*).

From among the pious predecessors, the first to adopt this path and to train his followers upon it was Khawāja Bahāʾ al-Dīn Naqshaband. He also gave it the name of perpetual contemplation (*dawām al-murāqaba*) and the name of specific direction (*wajha khāṣṣ*). One of the effects of this affinity is that it increases resolve and sharpness to the extent that the power of determination reaches the level of the 'Greatest Individual' (*al-shukhṣ al-akbar*). Increasing the resolve of those who have weak resolve, removing ailments and other abilities of this kind are only possible through this particular affinity. Knowing the state of the hearts of other people through disclosure (*kashf*) is also a fruit of this affinity.

5.5 THE AFFINITY OF EXTREME LOVE (NISBA AL-ʿISHQ)

The reality of this affinity is that when a believer has certitude of the fact that only Allah ﷻ is the possessor of all the qualities of perfection;

believes the remembrance of Allah ﷻ to be the cause of personal perfection; continues to perform the remembrance of Allah ﷻ while remembering His favours, then this continual performance of the remembrance of Allah (*dhikr*) and contemplation (*fikr*) over time creates restlessness, yearning and longing in the heart for Allah ﷻ.

This continuity in the remembrance of Allah (*dhikr*) gradually leads to the point that whenever the name of the Lord is uttered, such a state comes over the believer that it is as though the soul is about to leave the body. When this state takes hold in the lower self (*nafs*) of the believer and the lower self (*nafs*) is coloured in this state then this state is known as the affinity of extreme love.

Like other states of the lower self (*nafs*), the affinity of extreme love (*nisba al-ʿishq*) also takes hold in every part of the body of a believer. Intrinsic love also joins it. The combination of both of these creates a compound, the body of which is the affinity of extreme love (*nisba al-ʿishq*), and its soul is the intrinsic love. However, the person who experiences these states does not differentiate between the two.

A person who attains this affinity gains complete control of everything other than Allah ﷻ; and can also shun it all. This is the reason that the status of those who have this affinity is that whoever sees them treats them humbly and respectfully.

5.6 The Affinity of Ecstasy (Nisba al-Wajd)

Before understanding the reality of the affinity of ecstasy (*nisba al-wajd*), it is necessary to understand the rational self (*nafs nāṭiqa*) a little more. Whatever condition or state the rational self (*nafs nāṭiqa*) is in, it takes the qualities of those conditions. It will absorb influences of all conditions and states such as love, hate, anger, pleasure, fear, tranquillity, peace etc. Some of these are very pure angelic qualities while others are impure carnal qualities. When one of these states is effective upon it, then the conflicting state is automatically removed.

These states of the rational self (*nafs nāṭiqa*) are a result of different circumstances each of which has its own causes. When the seeker takes control of the causes that bring about and strengthen angelic and divine states then the rational self (*nafs nāṭiqa*) gains the ability to create these states. Then the rational self (*nafs nāṭiqa*) becomes so sensitive that very minute movements, which do not normally affect ordinary people, create an extra ordinary influence. A person whose rational self (*nafs nāṭiqa*) is sensitive in accepting angelic and divine effects, a minute initiation can have a lasting effect. However, if someone is by instinct dull minded and has a static temperament then, in that case, the creation of any subtle state in the rational self (*nafs nāṭiqa*) becomes almost impossible.

In order to create these types of states in the rational self (*nafs nāṭiqa*), such a person needs to have extreme love for someone, on the condition that this love is pure and does not involve carnal desires. To create these subtle states in the rational self (*nafs nāṭiqa*), there is the need for such a person to take part in spiritual Sufi music. These sittings must be pure sittings, conducted according to the set etiquettes, engaged in singing the praises of Allah ﷻ and the Holy Prophet ﷺ along with mystical poetry that expresses divine love, beauty and gnosis. This helps in removing the static quality of this type of the lower self (*nafs*).

However, in this regard, the Holy Prophet ﷺ has recommended a path for the seekers of ecstasy (*wajd*). That is, reciting and listening to the Holy Qur'ān and listening to appropriate sermons and advice. Attention should be paid to the meaning of the Holy Qur'ān. Its recitation should be listened to with complete concentration and longing. Paying attention to the meaning, wherever there is mention of Allah's forgiveness and mercy, one should seek it and where punishment is mentioned, forgiveness should be sought. Where Allah's attributes are mentioned, Allah ﷻ should be praised. Besides this, Prophetic traditions and stories of Saints that create inner softness and ecstasy should be read. The meanings given by them should be repeatedly recalled to mind.

These are not the only ways of removing temperamental rigidity and making the rational self (*nafs nāṭiqa*) receptive but there are also many other ways. Sometimes viewing powerful waves in rivers, seas and oceans and the endless vastness of deserts and valleys or by a thought occurring in the mind which refreshes the memory of a specific spiritual state, can create this state. In the same way, listening to some subtle spiritual discourse can create an ecstatic state.

According to the people of spiritual excellence, the affinity of ecstasy (*nisba al-wajd*) has an outer and an inner. The outer refers to the state of ecstasy taking hold in every part of the body. Its inner reality is that the soul (*rūḥ*), after gaining one gnosis, gains another gnosis and after becoming annihilated in one of the names of Allah ﷻ, then gets annihilated in another of His divine names.

Those who obtain this affinity, a vast majority of them are extremely fond of Sufi music. Those out of them who are upon the 'station of annihilation and permanence' (*fanāʾ wa baqāʾ*), such realities and gnoses appear to them that cannot be described.

5.7 The Affinity of Divine Oneness (Nisba al-Tawḥīd)

The reality of this affinity is that amongst people there are those who are greatly affected by the command of Being. It is in the nature of their temperament that they see all things in the universe to be annihilated in the Necessary Being (*wājib al-wujūd*) i.e. Allah ﷻ. They see the Necessary Being inside all things and they also feel that whatever is in the universe is dependent upon the necessary being for its existence.

The feeling of annihilation gradually eliminates one's knowledge and awareness of other existences. In their mind, they see other things, but this feeling grows to the extent that the day comes where they perceive that there is nothing else except the one existence. This feeling burns away everything else and renders upon them a condition whereby they cease to remember anything else. At the time of need, however, their minds are provided with the imprints of the commands of other levels of existence. Even when they acknowledge something, after the need for it goes, it quickly vanishes from their minds. The natural inclination of their temperament always prevails and eliminates their knowledge of other states of existence. At the start, the seeker perceives the existence of the reality, i.e. Allah ﷻ, inside everything. Gradually this feeling and perception becomes a natural disposition. The seeker becomes fully coloured with the colour of this disposition.

This can be further explained using the example of a person who through contemplation reaches the conclusion that all things are annihilated into one being which exists inside all things. By recalling this result continually in the mind, it takes the form of a natural disposition which then colours the person with its colour. However, the point of unveiling does not awaken. So the attraction of the knowledge of the being and the seeker being totally engrossed in it could not bring the seeker to that level where the natural disposition of this knowledge settles into the root of the lower self (*nafs*) of the seeker. The example of such a seeker is that of a pond which suddenly becomes full of water from a flood. It is not that water which comes slowly from different places, but it was a flood that swept in suddenly and filled it.

The seeker believing in the Being in this way is 'Theoretical *Tawḥīd*' (*al-tawḥīd al-ʿilmī*). This *tawḥīd*, in the form of knowledge of the being (*ʿilm al-wujūd*), goes beyond the body of the Seeker and awakens the very reality of the being of the human. It does it in a way that a direct connection is created with the divine being and as a result various effects start to appear, such as the veils of creation being removed. This kind is known as 'Experiential *Tawḥīd*' (*al-tawḥīd al-ḥālī*). When this effect of Divine Oneness (*tawḥīd*) settles strongly, it is called the affinity of *tawḥīd* (*nisba al-tawḥīd*). It is at this point where the seeker sees the real meaning of '*Kullu shayʾ hālikun illā wajhuhu*' (Everything perishes except His Countenance).

6

THE SEVEN TYPES OF THE LOWER SELF

Just like Allah ﷻ has created the intellect (*ʿaql*), heart (*qalb*) and soul (*ruh*) inside the human being, He has also created the lower self (*nafs*) as an independent reality. It has seven levels referred to as the 'seven selves' (*nufūs*). Each one has its own unique attributes and influences that are apparent from one's temperament, moral behaviour and deeds. The lower self (*nafs*) also has its own influence on the formation of states and conditions upon the human heart and soul. This is why the entire struggle for spiritual development involves the purification of the lower self (*tazkiya al-nafs*). It is for this reason that the Holy Prophet ﷺ declared the process of purification of the lower self as the 'greater struggle' (*al-jihād al-akbar*).

6.1 The Commanding Self (al-Nafs al-Ammāra)

This is the first of the seven levels. It is the most inciting towards sin and drags one towards worldly desires. It entices the person towards indecency, immorality, base desires and evil deeds. In the Holy Qur'ān, it is stated regarding it:

﴿إِنَّ ٱلنَّفْسَ لَأَمَّارَةٌۢ بِٱلسُّوٓءِ﴾

Certainly, the self commands much evil.[150]

[150] Qur'ān 12:53.

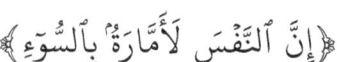

6.1.1 The Characteristics of the Commanding Self

Among the characteristics of the 'Commanding Self' (*al-nafs al-ammāra*) are:

- Stinginess
- Greed
- Being covetous
- Evil deeds
- Controlled by base desires
- Foolishness
- Hatred
- Jealousy
- Animosity
- Ignorance
- Negligence
- Laziness
- Anger
- Backbiting
- Slandering

Having even a single one of these bad character traits is evidence of the Commanding Self (*al-nafs al-ammāra*).

A few examples of the attributes of the Commanding Self (*al-nafs al-ammāra*) from the Holy Qur'ān are presented below. Allah ﷻ states in the Holy Qur'ān:

﴿أَفَكُلَّمَا جَآءَكُمْ رَسُولٌۢ بِمَا لَا تَهْوَىٰٓ أَنفُسُكُمُ ٱسْتَكْبَرْتُمْ﴾

> *Whenever a messenger comes to you and brings what you do not like you adopt arrogance.*[151]

Here, arrogance, a prevalent attribute of the Commanding Self (*al-nafs al-ammāra*), is mentioned. The rejection of the truth is also mentioned to be caused by this level of the lower self (*nafs*). It is further stated:

---

151 Qur'ān 2:87.

﴿وَمَن يَرۡغَبُ عَن مِّلَّةِ إِبۡرَٰهِـۧمَ إِلَّا مَن سَفِهَ نَفۡسَهُۥ﴾

Who will turn away from the dīn of Ibrāhīm except for someone who has ignorance and foolishness?[152]

In this verse, two attributes of the Commanding Self (*al-nafs al-ammāra*) have been mentioned: ignorance and foolishness. The carnal inclinations of the lower self (*nafs*) are mentioned in the Holy Qur'ān as follows:

﴿زُيِّنَ لِلنَّاسِ حُبُّ ٱلشَّهَوَٰتِ مِنَ ٱلنِّسَآءِ وَٱلۡبَنِينَ وَٱلۡقَنَٰطِيرِ
ٱلۡمُقَنطَرَةِ مِنَ ٱلذَّهَبِ وَٱلۡفِضَّةِ وَٱلۡخَيۡلِ ٱلۡمُسَوَّمَةِ وَٱلۡأَنۡعَٰمِ وَٱلۡحَرۡثِۗ
ذَٰلِكَ مَتَٰعُ ٱلۡحَيَوٰةِ ٱلدُّنۡيَاۖ وَٱللَّهُ عِندَهُۥ حُسۡنُ ٱلۡمَـَٔابِ﴾

(Excessively) attractive has been made, for the people, the love of lusts (that) include women, children, and hoarded treasures of gold and silver, and branded horses and cattle and crops. (All) this is the provision of the worldly life and with Allah is the best abode.[153]

6.1.2 THE METAPHORICAL FORMS OF THE COMMANDING SELF IN DREAMS

Each level of the lower self (*nafs*) can be easily identified by the seeker (*sālik*) through dreams. Each of the seven selves (*nafs*) can be seen in dreams according to their dominant conditions and its states appearing in distinct forms. Many people, in their dreams, see their own self (*nafs*) taking on various forms. They do not, however, realise that the form they have seen is in fact the state of their own self (*nafs*). By knowing the meaning of the forms, it will be possible to identify one's level. Some of the forms that refer to the Commanding Self (*al-nafs al-ammāra*) are:

- Swine

---

152 Qur'ān 2:130.

153 Qur'ān 3:14.

- Dog
- Elephant
- Snake
- Donkey
- Scorpion
- Mouse
- Flea
- Lice
- Sparrow or any bird

Seeing any of these in a dream is evidence of the Commanding Self (*al-nafs al-ammāra*).

In addition to these, seeing the following in a dream is also evidence of this state:

- Toilet room
- Stable
- Alcohol
- Opium or drugs, or any other intoxicant
- Dirty water
- Mud
- Standing water, such as a pond
- Flowing water of black or murky colour

If any of these are seen, then they are the specific qualities of the Commanding Self (*al-nafs al-ammāra*). These forms inform the individual concerned that they are at the level of the Commanding Self (*al-nafs al-ammāra*).

6.1.3 Interpretation of the Metaphorical Forms

The following are some interpretations of the above metaphorical forms:

- Seeing a pig in a dream is indicative of an unlawful (*ḥarām*) attribute.
- To see a dog in a dream is indicative of anger and rage being a dominant trait.
- Seeing an elephant indicates pride and arrogance.

- Seeing a snake is a sign of hypocrisy.
- A scorpion is a sign of torment.
- Birds, flees or lice refer to disliked (*makrūh*) things or undesirable habits.
- Toilets are a sign of being consumed by the love of the material world.
- Drinking or tasting alcohol is a sign of the person being engaged in unlawful (*ḥarām*) acts.
- Seeing alcohol, but not drinking it, refers to unlawful (*ḥarām*) intentions or thoughts.
- To see pubs or bars refers to corrupt thoughts.

The seeker (*sālik*) seeing any of these means that the lower self (*nafs*) is at the level of the Commanding Self (*al-nafs al-ammāra*). The required action must be taken in order remedy the specific dominating attribute referred to in the dream.

In the terminology of *taṣawwuf*, the heart of someone who is dominated by the Commanding Self (*al-nafs al-ammāra*) is known as the 'animalistic heart', as the temperament and disposition of such a person are dominated by animalistic qualities. Such a heart receives satanic whispering and negative thoughts. Sometimes, the state of the heart is so bad that satanic whispers are created within the heart and mind without external influence. Sometimes, the satanic whispering is so strong that it is not considered to be whispering but as the person's own thoughts, which are accepted by the mind as that. They then develop into systems of belief, and in the end, the satanic whispering lends to doubts. Then, gradually progressing on this path, such a person becomes so engrossed in sin that the person becomes an embodiment of the Commanding Self (*al-nafs al-ammāra*). It loses any sense of fairness, piety and moderation.

6.1.4 EFFECTIVE INVOCATIONS FOR THE COMMANDING SELF – THE FIRST LITANY (WAẒĪFA)

The effective invocation (*dhikr*) to gain freedom from the Commanding Self (*al-nafs al-ammāra*) is to recite '*lā ilāha illā Allāh*' (There is no god but Allah) 500,000 times.

Getting permission from the *Shaykh*, it should be completed 500,000 times with complete discipline and consistency. Alongside this, it is necessary to adhere to all obligatory (*farḍ*) and compulsory (*wājib*) requirements, as well as abiding by the rulings of the Sharia. Furthermore, supererogatory worship, repentance and charity should be performed as much as possible. The method of performing the invocation (*dhikr*) of '*lā ilāha illā Allāh*' has been detailed in a previous chapter.

In order to purify the lower self (*nafs*) of evil character traits, during the performance of this litany, which involves negation and affirmation, the following points should be adopted to improve concentration:

1. During the first 100,000 repetition, the concentration of the heart and mind should be on the following meaning:

   لَا مَعبُودَ إِلَّا اللهُ.

   There is no deity, but Allah ﷻ.

   During the performance of this invocation, while negating every '*ilāh*' except Allah ﷻ, the meaning of '*ilāh*' should be taken as '*maʿbūd*' i.e. deity. Every time this litany is recited, all deities besides Allah ﷻ should be negated from the heart and mind.

2. During the second 100,000 repetition, the concentration of the heart and mind should be on the following meaning:

   لَا مَطْلُوبَ إِلَّا اللهُ.

   There is none needed, but Allah ﷻ.

   Every pursuit for anything besides Allah ﷻ is negated. Thus, the heart and mind are purified of any desire for anything other Him ﷻ.

3. During the third 100,000 repetition, the concentration of the heart and mind should be on the following meaning:

   لَا مَحْبُوبَ إِلَّا اللهُ.

   There is no beloved, but Allah ﷻ.

While negating every *'ilāh'* except Allah ﷻ, the meaning of *'ilāh'* should be taken as *'maḥbūb'* i.e. beloved. By doing this gradually, love for everything other than Allah ﷻ will be removed from the heart.

4. During the fourth 100,000 repetition, the concentration of the heart and mind should be on the following meaning:

لَا مَقْصُودَ إِلَّا اللهُ.

There is no objective, but Allah ﷻ.

The performance of this invocation will increase one's focus and remove one's attention from all things besides Allah ﷻ.

5. During the fifth 100,000 repetition, the concentration of the heart and mind should be on the following meaning:

لَا مَوْجُودَ إِلَّا اللهُ.

There is no existent, but Allah ﷻ.

Every other existence other than Allah ﷻ is to be negated. Gradually, everything that comes under 'other than Allah ﷻ' is removed from the heart and mind.

The practical method of doing this can be by meditating on the invocation before performing the focus invocation for a hundred thousand times. When this meaning of the focus name is dominant then the invocation can be performed.

With this method, the essence of Divine Oneness (*tawḥīd*) will shine, and by its lights the lower self (*nafs*) will begin to become purified. In order to strengthen the concentration upon the five focus invocations and to receive their lights and blessings, the focus invocations should also be repeated and performed as a litany. In this manner, the lower self (*nafs*) will break free from the Commanding Self (*al-nafs al-ammāra*) and progress to the next level.

6.1.5 Performing the Litany (Waẓīfa) in Seclusion

If this litany is performed in seclusion, then the invocation of *'lā ilāha illā Allāh'* (There is no God but Allah) is to be performed only 70,000 times.

6.1.6 Tabular Outline for the Commanding Self

The Sufi Imams have made a table consisting of the stations of the invocations and attributes of the seven levels of the lower self (*nafs*). Only some vital points have been taken from it and presented below. This is only for the benefit of the scholars, and not the general public who should not delve into such delicate matters.

The Commanding Self (*al-Nafs al-Ammāra*)	Details
Its journey (*safr*)...	is towards Allah ﷻ (*ilā Allāh*)
Its realm (*ʿālam*)...	is the physical realm (*shahāda/nāsūt*)
Its locus (*maḥal*)...	is the chest
Its state (*ḥāl*)...	is of inclination and longing
Its inrush (*wārid*)...	is the outward of the Sharia
Its light (*nūr*)...	is blue

6.2 The Condemning Self (al-Nafs al-Lawwāma)

The Condemning Self (*al-nafs al-lawwāma*) is the second level of the lower self (*nafs*). After successfully progressing from the Commanding Self (*al-nafs al-ammāra*), the lower self (*nafs*) upgrades to the Condemning Self (*al-nafs al-lawwāma*). At this stage, a light comes into being in the heart which becomes a source of internal guidance. When a person possessing this level of the lower self (*nafs*) commits a sin or transgresses, the Condemning Self (*al-nafs al-lawwāma*) immediately starts to condemn and rebuke the person. For this reason, it is called the 'Condemning Self' or the 'Reproaching Self'. It is a good level of the lower self (*nafs*), not only because it differentiates between good and evil, but also because it instils hatred for what is bad.

Allah ﷻ has sworn by it in the Holy Qur'ān:

﴿لَآ أُقْسِمُ بِيَوْمِ ٱلْقِيَـٰمَةِ وَلَآ أُقْسِمُ بِٱلنَّفْسِ ٱللَّوَّامَةِ﴾

I swear by the Day of Resurrection. And I swear by the blaming self, reproaching (itself for evil deeds).[154]

This level of the lower self (*nafs*) is bestowed to the righteous and those who practise their knowledge. The following verse also refers to it:

﴿وَأَمَّا مَنْ خَافَ مَقَامَ رَبِّهِۦ وَنَهَى ٱلنَّفْسَ عَنِ ٱلْهَوَىٰ ۝ فَإِنَّ ٱلْجَنَّةَ هِىَ ٱلْمَأْوَىٰ﴾

But as for him who feared standing in the presence of his Lord and forbade (his ill-commanding) self its appetites and lusts, Paradise will surely be (his) abode.[155]

In this regard, the following verse about the story of Prophet Yūsuf ﷺ is also of relevance:

﴿وَمَآ أُبَرِّئُ نَفْسِىٓ ۚ إِنَّ ٱلنَّفْسَ لَأَمَّارَةٌۢ بِٱلسُّوٓءِ إِلَّا مَا رَحِمَ رَبِّىٓ ۚ﴾

And I do not (claim) absolution of myself. Certainly, the self commands much evil except the one on whom my Lord bestows mercy.[156]

In other words, the restraint of the lower self (*nafs*) from sin and evil actually entails that it has liberated itself from the Commanding Self (*al-nafs al-ammāra*).

6.2.1 THE CHARACTERISTICS OF THE CONDEMNING SELF

Among the characteristics of the 'Condemning Self' (*al-nafs al-lawwāma*) are:

- Inclination towards the lawful (*ḥalāl*)
- Inclination towards benefitting people
- To relieve others of their burden
- To avoid frivolous and immoral things
- Righteous morals

[154] Qur'ān 75:1-2.

[155] Qur'ān 79:40-41.

[156] Qur'ān 12:53.

Although this is a higher station of the lower self (*nafs*), it still has some undesirable qualities for which purification (*tazkiya*) is required. Such qualities include:

- Deceit
- Greed
- Conceit
- Pride and arrogance
- Creating unmerited and undue objections
- Showing rage and being violent
- Carnal desires

6.2.2 The Metaphorical Forms of the Condemning Self in Dreams

The metaphorical forms seen in dreams that are evidence of the 'Condemning Self' (*al-nafs al-lawwāma*) include:

- Sheep
- Goat
- Cow
- Camel
- Fish
- Pigeon
- Duck
- Chicken
- Tree
- Dates
- Cooked food
- Fruit
- Clothes
- Saddleless horse
- Extinguished lamp
- Lights or candles
- Bread
- Shops
- Buildings or mansions
- Honey

- Sugar cane
- Sweet drinks

If one of these particular things are seen, then it is evidence of the 'Condemning Self' (*al-nafs al-lawwāma*).

6.2.3 INTERPRETATION OF THE METAPHORICAL FORMS

The following are some interpretations of the metaphorical forms seen in dreams:

- Goats and sheep are an indication of inclining towards the lawful (*ḥalāl*).
- The quality of a cow is to work and benefit people, while the qualities of a camel is to carry the burden of others and to tolerate hardship. Adopting these qualities is a sign of faith (*īmān*).
- To see a fish, pigeon, duck, chicken and other pure and *ḥalāl* animals also refers to an inclination towards the lawful (*ḥalāl*).
- Dates and honey refer to desirable moral conduct.
- Cooked food refers to the desires of the lower self (*nafs*).
- Fruit refers to the need to dispense of frivolous talk.
- Buildings and dwellings refer to the lower self (*nafs*) desiring luxury.

In summary, the qualities of the various things seen in dreams, such as the animals and birds, refer to the condition of the lower self (*nafs*). This then enables individuals to ascertain the good and bad states of their lower self (*nafs*). Using this knowledge, corrective measures can be taken to reform oneself and to take the next step to progress on the spiritual path.

The heart of the individual who is on the level of the 'Condemning Self' (*al-nafs al-lawwāma*) is known as the 'human heart' (*al-qalb al-insānī*). The Condemning Self (*al-nafs al-lawwāma*) can be likened, by way of example, to a rebellious horse. It is not fundamentally impure, but it is rebellious and requires a bridle to keep it under control. Meaning that when a horse is fully bridled, the rider is in control, and it can only go where the rider wants it to go. If it is not bridled, then the horse is in control, and it goes wherever it wants.

The question arises as to how the 'human heart' (*al-qalb al-insānī*) comes into existence? This can be easily understood as follows: when a person has a combination of angelic and animalistic qualities, i.e. pure and base qualities, then both of these are combined and synchronised in such a way that one's temperament settles into a balanced state. The inner reality of such a person is neither completely changed to light nor does it remain in complete darkness, rather it is between the two. Such a person fears Hell and desires Paradise. The actions performed by the person are moulded by this fear and desire. The heart of such a person is known as the 'forgetful heart' (*al-qalb al-insānī*) and the lower self (*nafs*) is known as the 'Condemning Self' (*al-nafs al-lawwāma*).

6.2.4 Effective Invocations for the Condemning Self – The Second Litany (Waẓīfa)

The prescribed invocation (*dhikr*) to break free from the Condemning Self (*al-nafs al-lawwāma*) is *'Allāh'*, which is known as the essential name (*ism al-dhāt*). It is more beneficial to perform it as *'yā Allāh'*. It is to be performed 500,000 times using the same method as given for the previous level of the lower self (*nafs*). All conditions and requirements must be met in order for the seeker to progress to the next level of the lower self (*nafs*).

During this litany, two particular focus invocations (*adhkār*) will prove useful. The first is:

يَا نُورُ يَا اَللهُ.

O Giver of Light! O Allah!

The second is:

يَا هَادِي يَا اَللهُ.

O Provider of Guidance! O Allah!

The essential name (*ism al-dhāt*) of Allah ﷻ is the actual invocation which is to be performed in the litany. In order to strengthen the concentration upon this litany, the above two invocations can also be recited repeatedly. The light from them assists with the litany.

6.2.5 Performing the Litany (Waẓīfa) in Seclusion

Performing this litany in seclusion requires for it to be performed only 60,000 times.

6.2.6 Tabular Outline for the Condemning Self

The following is a tabular outline for the Condemning Self (*al-nafs al-lawwāma*).

The Condemning Self (*al-Nafs al-Lawwāma*)	Details
Its journey (*safr*)...	is for Allah ﷻ (*li'Llāh*)
Its realm (*ʿālam*)...	is the intermediate realm (*barzakh*)
Its locus (*maḥal*)...	is the heart
Its state (*ḥāl*)...	is of love (*maḥabba*)
Its inrush (*wārid*)...	is the inward of the Sharia
Its light (*nūr*)...	is yellow

6.3 The Inspiring Self (al-Nafs al-Mulhima)

The Inspiring Self (*al-nafs al-mulhima*) is the third level of the lower self (*nafs*). It inspires thoughts of righteousness and obedience in the heart i.e. it send inspirations (*ilhām*). This is why it is given the name of the 'Inspiring Self' (*al-nafs al-mulhima*). Just as the Condemning Self (*al-nafs al-lawwāma*) creates animosity for sin due to its internal light, in the same way, the Inspiring Self (*al-nafs al-mulhima*), due to its internal light, inclines the heart and the temperament towards piety and vigilance to Allah (*taqwā*). This increases the inclination towards pious and righteous deeds.

The temperament of the one characterised with the Inspiring Self (*al-nafs al-mulhima*) becomes attached to pious and righteous deeds. If acts of worship are missed, then it induces a state of anxiety and sadness in the individual. The only way for the person to remove this constricted state is to perform deeds of piety and righteousness.

6.3.1 The Characteristics of the Inspiring Self

The prevalent attributes of the Inspiring Self (*al-nafs al-mulhima*) are:

- Contentment (*qanāʿa*)
- Generosity (*sakhāwa*)
- Knowledge (*ʻilm*)
- Humbleness and modesty (*tawāḍuʿ*)
- Repentance (*tawba*)
- Patience (*ṣabr*)
- Forbearance (*ḥilm*)
- Sincerity (*ikhlāṣ*)

At this level, righteous deeds, morals and conduct are prevalent in the attributes of the lower self (*nafs*).

6.3.2 The Metaphorical Forms of the Inspiring Self in Dreams

Seeing the following in dreams is evidence of the Inspiring Self (*al-nafs al-mulhima*):

- A disbeliever, atheist, an open sinner or someone with deviant beliefs
- Someone who is clean-shaven or has no beard
- A lame, deaf or dumb person
- An ecstatic or intoxicated person
- A transgender person
- A slave or a freed slave
- A soldier
- A spy
- A gambler
- A wrestler
- A jester or a clown
- A security guard
- Women
- A storyteller

- A butcher
- A broker
- A thief
- A person who makes excuses very well
- A squint-eyed person
- A blind person
- Somebody with tuberculosis
- A monkey

6.3.3 INTERPRETATION OF THE METAPHORICAL FORMS

The following are some interpretations of the metaphorical forms seen in dreams:

- Seeing a disbeliever or an atheist is a sign of something lacking with regards to one's religion (*dīn*).
- Seeing someone with deviant beliefs is a sign of a defect in one's beliefs.
- A clean-shaven person is a sign of defect and weakness with regards to practising the Sharia.
- Seeing a lame person is a sign of not being obedient to Allah ﷻ while one is inviting others towards Allah ﷻ.
- Seeing a person who does not have a beard is a sign of not carrying out divine injunctions.
- Seeing a blind man is a sign of hiding the truth.
- Seeing a deaf person is a sign of not wanting to listen to the teachings of the Sharia and ignoring them.
- Seeing a dumb person is a sign of one not speaking the truth.
- Seeing a slave is a sign of speaking ill of whoever one talks about meaning one does not talk about the good qualities of people.
- Seeing a spy is a sign of one not following the Sunna.
- To see an intoxicated person is a sign of one being involved in metaphorical worldly love.
- Seeing a gambler, wrestler, clown or storyteller is a sign one does not perform acts of worship and is involved in something unlawful (*ḥarām*).

- Seeing a thief is a sign of performing acts of worship for ostentation.
- Seeing a broker is a sign of one being a liar or one does not have pure eyes i.e. gazes at opposite gender.
- Seeing a butcher is a sign of darkness in one's heart.
- Seeing a blind or squint-eyed person is a sign of one being misguided.

It must be kept in mind that the sins and faults of an individual at this level are in-line with the person's own level, grade and state. The pious predecessors used to say:

حَسَنَاتُ الْأَبْرَارِ سَيِّئَاتُ الْمُقَرَّبِينَ.

The virtues of the righteous are the vices of the intimate.

That is, those who are blessed with the intimate presence of Allah ﷻ will not be content on sufficing on the good deeds of the common people. Performing good deeds like the common people would be deemed a shortcoming in their respect according to the requirement of their grade. For such people, who are among the elite, their level of the lower self (*nafs*) is the Inspiring Self (*al-nafs al-mulhima*), which is one level above the Condemning Self (*al-nafs al-lawamma*). Even the slightest blemish in their soul will be manifested metaphorically in dreams as major sins and defects.

The similarity between the metaphorical forms of these two levels of the lower self (*nafs*) is like a small particle that is magnified under a lens or a small blot on a clean white sheet. Normally, such miniscule defects would not be seen in normal situations but, in these particular situations, they are very much apparent and visible. Such is the similitude of the Inspiring Self (*al-nafs al-mulhima*) and the metaphorical forms in dreams. The more the lower self (*nafs*) increases in purity through continual purification (*tazkiya*), the minutest of baseness or sin appear more apparent. As the grade of these individuals increases their focus upon inner purification also increases.

6.3.4 Effective Invocations for the Inspiring Self – The Third Litany (Waẓīfa)

To progress from the Inspiring Self (*al-nafs al-mulhima*), the litany of '*hū*' (He) is to be performed. It is to be performed 500,000 times and it should be completed according to the method mentioned above following the permission of one's spiritual guide (*Shaykh*). While performing the invocation, being involved in worldly affiliations should be limited to a minimum and acts of worship should be increased, the details of which can be ascertained from the spiritual guide (*Shaykh*) at the time.

It is more effective to perform this litany with the following focus invocation:

يَا هُوَ أَنْتَ هُوَ.

O He [Allah ﷻ]! You are He!

It is also recommended to perform it together with repetitions of the following focus invocation, which will help in performing this litany for this level of the lower self:

يَا مَنْ لَا إِلَٰهَ إِلَّا هُوَ.

O the One Whom there is no God but Him!

6.3.5 Performing the Litany (Waẓīfa) in Seclusion

Performing this litany in seclusion requires for it to be performed only 50,000 times.

6.3.6 Tabular Outline for the Inspiring Self

The following is a tabular outline for the Inspiring Self (*al-nafs al-mulhima*).

The Condemning Self (*al-Nafs al-Lawwāma*)	Details
Its journey (*safr*)...	is dependent upon Allah ﷻ (*ʿalā Allāh*)
Its realm (*ʿālam*)...	is the realm of the souls (*ʿālam al-arwāḥ*)
Its locus (*maḥal*)...	is the soul
Its state (*ḥāl*)...	is of extreme love (*ʿishq*)
Its inrush (*wārid*)...	is the inner secrets of the Sharia
Its light (*nūr*)...	is red

6.4 The Contented Self (al-Nafs al-Muṭmaʾinna)

The Contented Self (*al-nafs al-muṭmaʾinna*) is the fourth level of the lower self (*nafs*). It is completely purified of vices and possesses only virtuous attributes. After creating a connection with the divine, it attains a state of internal fulfilment, which is why it is referred to as the 'Contented Self' (*al-nafs al-muṭmaʾinna*). Allah Almighty addresses this level of the lower self (*nafs*) in the Holy Qur'ān:

﴿يَٰٓأَيَّتُهَا ٱلنَّفْسُ ٱلْمُطْمَئِنَّةُ ۝٢٧ ٱرْجِعِىٓ إِلَىٰ رَبِّكِ رَاضِيَةً مَّرْضِيَّةً﴾

O contented (pleased) self! Return to your Lord in such a state that you are both the aspirant to, and the aspired of, His pleasure (i.e., you seek His pleasure, and He seeks yours).[157]

6.4.1 The Station of Sainthood (Wilāya)

The Contented Self (*al-nafs al-muṭmaʾinna*) is the level of the saints (*awliyāʾ*) and is the station known as the lesser sainthood (*al-wilāya al-ṣughrā*). When it is established, it leads to the station known as 'Annihilation in the Messenger ﷺ' (*fanāʾ fī al-Rasūl*).

Its reality is such that when a person gains strong angelic qualities by the blessing of Allah ﷻ – be it God given or acquired through worship and inner struggle – and the animalistic qualities are reduced

[157] Qur'ān 89:27-28.

to a minimal level and brought under complete control to the extent that it is as though they never existed, the spiritual heart (*qalb*) goes up to the grade of the spirit (*rūḥ*) and the lower self (*nafs*) moves up to the grade of the spiritual heart (*qalb*). The unique feature of the spiritual heart (*qalb*) is that it finds contentment in the remembrance (*dhikr*) of Allah ﷻ, as Allah Almighty states in the Holy Qur'ān:

﴿ٱلَّذِينَ ءَامَنُواْ وَتَطۡمَئِنُّ قُلُوبُهُم بِذِكۡرِ ٱللَّهِۗ أَلَا بِذِكۡرِ ٱللَّهِ تَطۡمَئِنُّ ٱلۡقُلُوبُ﴾

> *Those who believe and their hearts become calm and contented with the remembrance of Allah—know that it is the remembrance of Allah alone that brings calm to the hearts.*[158]

When the lower self (*nafs*) moves up to the grade of the spiritual heart (*qalb*), the spiritual heart (*qalb*) is already engaged in the remembrance of Allah (*dhikr*) because it has progressed from the levels of the Commanding Self, the Condemning Self and then the Inspiring Self. As the spiritual heart (*qalb*) gradually becomes satisfied by the remembrance of Allah ﷻ, its contentment starts to become an independent state of the lower self (*nafs*). This is the reason that the lower self (*nafs*) changes into the spiritual heart (*qalb*) and becomes the Contented Self (*al-nafs al-muṭma'inna*). As far as the spiritual heart (*qalb*) is concerned, as it has been previously stated, it gains the grade of the soul (*rūḥ*).

With the spiritual heart (*qalb*) being at the grade of the soul (*rūḥ*), there is no need for extensive inner struggle and worship to gain inner purification (*tazkiya*). The inner purification (*tazkiya*) and spiritual state can be secured by merely performing the daily acts of worship. However, to progress spiritually and to achieve the higher levels of the lower self (*nafs*), extensive worship and litanies must be performed.

With respect to the soul (*rūḥ*), and it being 'from the divine command', it is stated in the Holy Qur'ān:

---

[158] Qur'ān 13:28.

﴿وَيَسْـَٔلُونَكَ عَنِ ٱلرُّوحِ ۖ قُلِ ٱلرُّوحُ مِنْ أَمْرِ رَبِّى وَمَآ أُوتِيتُم مِّنَ ٱلْعِلْمِ إِلَّا قَلِيلًا﴾

And they (the disbelievers) ask you about the soul. Say: 'The soul is from my Lord's command, and you have been given but a very little knowledge.'[159]

Therefore, when the spiritual heart (*qalb*) is at the grade of the soul (*rūḥ*), it is always subservient to the command of Allah ﷻ and continues to receive blessings from it. Now, without undergoing any contraction (*qabḍ*), the heart experiences the state of expansion (*basṭ*). Without any anxiety or disturbance, the heart remains satiated from the springs of love. Without becoming unconscious, it remains in the state of ecstasy (*wajd*). When the spiritual heart (*qalb*) progresses to the grade of the soul (*rūḥ*), then the soul progresses to the grade of the 'inner secret' (*sirr*).

In summary, the lower self (*nafs*) becomes the spiritual heart (*qalb*), the spiritual heart becomes the soul (*rūḥ*) and the soul changes to the 'inner secret' (*sirr*). At this point, the doors to the knowledge (*ʿilm*), gnosis (*maʿārif*) and secrets (*asrār*) of the realm of the unseen are opened. The person begins to receive knowledge, gnosis, secrets, realities and subtleties through non-conventional means. It is not acquired through the help of books, apparent insight or comprehension, nor from contemplation, spiritual disclosure (*kashf*) or from a voice from the unseen. Rather the soul (*rūḥ*) receives gnosis directly from the grade of the 'inner secret' (*sirr*) and then transfers it to the spiritual heart (*qalb*) (which is at the grade of the soul (*rūḥ*)). This is an unseen, unperceivable door of lights and secrets, the opening of which gives access to divinely infused knowledge (*al-ʿilm al-ladunnī*, i.e. inspired knowledge of secrets and gnosis). Any thought that enters the heart is completely in-line with the straight path (*al-ṣirāṭ al-mustaqīm*) and the person's deeds are righteous, his spoken words are blessed, and his supplications are accepted. This is the lesser sainthood (*al-wilāya al-ṣughrā*). The person does not perform miracles or actions of a supernatural nature but has the ability to do so.

---

[159] Qur'ān 17:85.

6.4.2 THE OPENING OF THE TWO PATHS

When a seeker, who is upon the lesser sainthood (*al-wilāya al-ṣughrā*), progresses, two paths become available to him. The two paths are:

1. The path of the greater sainthood
2. The path of prophetic inheritance

Some people receive spiritual blessings from one path and progress on either of the two paths, but there are others who are blessed with receiving blessings from both.

The path of the greater sainthood (*al-wilāya al-kubrā*) leads to the stations of the 'Poles' (*quṭbiyya*) and the 'Helpers' (*ghawthiyya*). The path of prophetic inheritance is the path of 'renewal' (*tajdīd*) and 'revival' (*iḥyā'*); those who are established on it are designated as 'revivalists' (*mujaddidīn*), and they are the vicegerents and inheritors of the Holy Prophet Muhammad ﷺ.

The person who is on the level of the Contented Self (*al-nafs al-muṭma'inna*), while being on the lesser sainthood (*al-wilāya al-ṣughrā*), inclines towards one of the two mentioned paths. The one who attains the greater sainthood (*al-wilāya al-kubrā*) will manifest miracles due to the advancement in spirituality. The one who takes to the path of prophetic inheritance becomes a source of guidance for people, and through him, societal evils begin to be eradicated. Through the struggle of the revivalist (*mujaddid*), there is an advancement of knowledge, reformation of the souls and the revival of Islam. These are the signs that the individual is upon the station of the revivalists (*mujaddidiyya*). Through these manifestations and signs, certainty about the two paths is gained.

The reality of the revivalist (*mujaddid*) being the vicegerent of the Messenger of Allah ﷺ is that the religious and moral state of the people of his time declined so much, that had it been in the era of the former communities, such a decline would have warranted another Prophet or Messenger to be sent to rectify the people. Due to the finality of Prophethood of the Holy Prophet Muhammad ﷺ and his being the last Prophet and Messenger of God, when such a situation arises in his nation (*umma*), it is impossible for a new Prophet to come. Instead, a revivalist (*mujaddid*) is born, who is the vicegerent of the Holy Prophet

Muhammad ﷺ. The revivalist performs the same duty as the Prophets in the earlier times before the Holy Prophet Muhammad ﷺ, which is why they are called the 'Inheritors of the Prophets'.

The Holy Prophet ﷺ stated:

إِنَّ الْعُلَمَاءَ وَرَثَةُ الْأَنْبِيَاءِ.

> Indeed, the scholars are the inheritors of the Prophets.[160]

He ﷺ also stated:

عُلَمَاءُ أُمَّتِي كَأَنْبِيَاءِ بَنِي إِسْرَائِيلَ.

> The scholars of my nation are like the Prophets of the Israelites (Banī Isrā'īl).[161]

Another reason for them being referred to as the 'Inheritors of the Prophets' is that they have been given the duty of revival (*tajdīd*) in place of prophethood (*nubuwwa*). They receive all the blessings from the light of the Holy Prophet Muhammad's Messengership (*risāla*).

This discussion should suffice on the Contented Self (*al-nafs al-muṭma'inna*) and its grade, and on sainthood (*wilāya*) and the paths that open to it.

Shāh Walī Allāh Muḥaddith Dihlawī discusses the two paths as:

1. The path of prophethood (*ṭarīq al-nubuwwa*)
2. The path of sainthood (*ṭarīq al-wilāya*)

Explaining the difference between the two, he states that the path of prophethood (*ṭarīq al-nubuwwa*) contains all-encompassing and complete excellence and perfection whereas the path of sainthood (*ṭarīq al-wilāya*) contains partial excellence and perfection. The peak of the path of sainthood (*ṭarīq al-wilāya*) are the stations of the 'Poles' (*quṭbiyya*) and the 'Helpers' (*ghawthiyya*) whereas the peak of the path of prophethood (*ṭarīq al-nubuwwa*) is prophetic inheritance and the

---

160 Narrated by Abū Dāwūd in *al-Sunan*: *Kitāb al-Aqḍiya* [The Book of Judgements], chapter: 'Encouragement of seeking knowledge', 3:317 §3641.

161 Narrated by Mullā ʿAlī al-Qārī in *al-Mirqāt al-Mafātīḥ*, 5:6223.

station of the revivalists (*mujaddidiyya*).

The station of the revivalists is above all stations of sainthood (*wilāya*) because a revivalist (*mujaddid*) is not only always spiritually focussed upon Allah ﷻ but, keeping this connection intact, delivers the blessings of Allah ﷻ to the *umma* by following the Holy Prophet's example (*sunna*). A revivalist (*mujaddid*) reaches the destination of perfection through the path of prophethood (*nabuwwa*). The grade and station of a revivalist (*mujaddid*) is far higher than the one of sainthood (*wilāya*). The reason for this is that compliance to the Sunna provides guidance at every step, from the beginning of the journey till arrival. It is like a beacon of light that leads to the destination upon the path of perfection.

During this discussion, Shāh Walī Allāh also solved the delicate issue of the superiority of the *Shaykhayn* (i.e. Abū Bakr and 'Umar ☙). He says:

"Do you know why Caliphs Abū Bakr and 'Umar ☙ have superiority over Caliph 'Alī ☙ – despite Caliph 'Alī ☙ being the first Sufi, *majdhūb*[162] and Gnostic ('*ārif*) in the *umma* and that other Companions do not have these particular perfections but only have a small part of them due to their connection with the Holy Prophet ﷺ?

I presented this question to the Holy Prophet ﷺ, and I was given the answer. What appeared to me is that the comprehensive superiority (*al-faḍl al-kullī*) according to the Holy Prophet ﷺ is that which performs the duties of prophethood such as the propagation of Islam and knowledge, together with ruling over the hearts of people and other related matters. The superiority that is related to the matter of sainthood (*wilāya*) like divine attraction (*jadhb*) and annihilation (*fanā'*) is only partial superiority and there is an angle of weakness in it. Caliphs Abū Bakr and 'Umar ☙ (*Shaykhayn*) are attributed to the first-comprehensive superiority so much so that I see them as a form of a spring from which water gushes out. The favours of Allah ﷻ that appeared on the Holy Prophet ﷺ also appeared on them. In terms of their perfections, they are at such a level of merit and virtue which are established with their essence, the realisation of which completes it. For that reason, even though Caliph 'Alī ☙ is closer to the Holy Prophet

---

[162] Someone who is absorbed in divine attraction (*jadhb*). Ed.

ﷺ in terms of lineage, his life and his nature than Caliphs Abū Bakr and ʿUmar ؓ and the fact that he is stronger in divine attraction (*jadhb*) and gnosis (*maʿrifa*) than them, the Holy Prophet ﷺ in terms of prophetic perfection is far more inclined towards Caliphs Abū Bakr and ʿUmar ؓ. For this reason, those scholars who are acquainted to the secrets (*maʿārif*) of prophethood attach superiority to Caliphs Abū Bakr and ʿUmar ؓ. Whereas those who are acquainted to the secrets of sainthood (*wilāya*) attach superiority to Caliph ʿAlī ؓ. For this reason, Caliphs Abū Bakr and ʿUmar ؓ are buried next to the Holy Prophet ﷺ."[163]

This is why Caliphs Abū Bakr and ʿUmar ؓ, despite possessing the light of sainthood (*wilāya*), focused more on the promotion and establishment of the *dīn* (i.e. Islam). Whereas Caliph ʿAlī ؓ, despite possessing the light of prophethood (*nubuwwa*), focused more on the promotion of spirituality (*rūḥāniyya*) and sainthood (*wilāya*), and it is for this reason that many of the spiritual orders (*ṭuruq*) start with him.

6.4.3 The Characteristics of the Contented Self

The prevalent attributes of the Contented Self (*al-nafs al-muṭmaʾinna*) are:

- Forgiveness and clemency
- Generosity
- Reliance upon Allah ﷻ
- Forbearance
- Worshipful servitude to Allah ﷻ
- Thankfulness and gratitude
- Being content

6.4.4 The Metaphorical Forms of the Contented Self in Dreams

Seeing the following in dreams is evidence of the Contented Self (*al-nafs al-muṭmaʾinna*):

- Recitation of the Holy Qur'ān

---

[163] Shāh Walī Allāh, *Fuyūḍ al-Ḥaramayn*, *mashhad*: 22.

- Prophets
- The Kaʿba, the Prophet's Mosque, the holy city of Madina or Jerusalem (*Bayt al-Maqdis*)
- A king, judge, scholar, *Shaykh* or saint (*walī*)
- Visiting a mosque, seminary (*madrasa*), homes of righteous people or sacred places
- A bow, arrow, sword, dagger or gun
- Books

It should be noted that sometimes other people, coincidentally, also see these things in their dreams, the interpretations for which will be different according to their individual spiritual states. These dreams are not evidence of the Contented Self (*al-nafs al-muṭmaʾinna*). The reason being that the attributes of the lower self (*nafs*) are key, so along with the dream, the attributes of the lower self (*nafs*) must also be examined and taken into consideration. If the aforementioned attributes are found in the lower self (*nafs*), then the dream can be evidence of the Contented Self (*al-nafs al-muṭmaʾinna*). Otherwise, every dream has its own interpretation. This is a delicate matter because sometimes a common sinful person may see Prophets or the pious predecessors in their dreams. They can have virtuous dreams, but this does not mean that they are at the level of the Contented Self (*al-nafs al-muṭmaʾinna*).

The reality behind this is that the lower self (*nafs*) receives a temporary theophany (*tajallī*) due to a special time or reason that holds partial and temporary resemblance to the states of the Contented Self (*al-nafs al-muṭmaʾinna*). Examples of acts that can cause this are giving charity, performing the *Ḥajj* or *ʿUmra*, worshipping greatly in the nights of *Layla al-Qadr* and *Layla al-Barāʾa* followed by crying and repentance, helping an oppressed person, serving parents and making them happy, looking at a saint or a pious scholar, reciting the Holy Qur'ān abundantly and attending a *dhikr* circle or a *mawlid* event etc.

When performing a virtuous act, the light of that action enters the lower self (*nafs*) and this temporarily increases the state of faith (*īmān*). Thus, a partial temporary resemblance is gained with the angelic states of the Contented Self (*al-nafs al-muṭmaʾinna*), which is witnessed in the form of a virtuous dream. Later that state does not remain because the level of the lower self (*nafs*) is not the Contented Self (*al-nafs al-muṭmaʾinna*) but is either of the Commanding Self (*al-nafs al-ammāra*), the Condemning Self (*al-nafs al-lawwāma*) or the Inspiring Self (*al-nafs al-mulhima*). This feeling is like a flash that is experienced by a Muslim on and off; it comes and goes according to the individual's state. The qualities and attributes of the lower self (*nafs*) that are discussed here are stable states, not temporary or coincidental ones. The dreams for each level of the lower self (*nafs*) are also permanent. So, to determine the level of the lower self (*nafs*) through dreams, comparison with the specific metaphorical forms that are mentioned for each level is required.

6.4.5 Interpretation of the Metaphorical Forms

The following are some interpretations of the metaphorical forms seen in dreams:

- To see the Holy Qur'ān in a dream means purity of the spiritual heart (*qalb*). Seeing or reciting a chapter or verse in a dream that corresponds to one's state also occurs on occasions. This can only be ascertained through the science of the interpretation of dreams. This is also an indication of pleasant news to come.
- To see the Prophets refers to the state of one's faith (*īmān*) and practice (*ʿamal*). Sometimes they are a source of guidance and sometimes they reflect one's state. At times, seeing them can be an indication towards the state of society or towards the current state of Islam and Muslims.
- Seeing a king is an indication towards the need of one to return to worship and inner struggle.
- To see extreme lovers of Allah ﷻ from among the saints (*awliyāʾ*) refers to being steadfast in worship and towards inner spiritual attention.
- To see a *Shaykh* is guidance for the lower self (*nafs*).
- To see a judge refers to compliance with the commandments (*aḥkām*) of Allah ﷻ.
- To see the *Kaʿba* and the holy city of Madina refers to being pure

from satanic whispering. This state can be judged by the state in which this is seen in the dream.

- A mosque where Friday prayers are conducted (*jāmiᶜ masjid*), a seminary (*madrasa*), a flag or banner, a bow and arrow, a gun and other firearms all refer to the presence of whispering in accordance with one's state. It is guidance to work further on their removal. It should be noted that this whispering can be from the lower self (*nafs*), the devil (*shayṭān*) and the spiritual heart (*qalb*), which come according to one's state. They are also removed in different ways.

6.4.6 Effective Invocations for the Contented Self – The Fourth Litany (Waẓīfa)

The effective invocation (*dhikr*) for this is the divine name *'al-Ḥaqq'* (the Ultimate Truth). Its litany is to be performed by repeating the following 500,000 times:

يَا حَقُّ أَنْتَ الْحَقُّ.

O the Ultimate Truth! You are the Truth!

The following two focus invocations should be used. The first is:

يَا مُجِيبُ أَنْتَ الْحَقُّ.

O One Who accepts supplications!
You are the Ultimate Truth!

The second is:

يَا مُغِيثُ أَنْتَ الْحَقُّ.

O Succourer! You are the Ultimate Truth!

6.4.7 Performing the Litany (Waẓīfa) in Seclusion

This litany should be performed only 40,000 times, if performed in seclusion.

6.4.8 Tabular Outline for the Contented Self

The following is a tabular outline for the Contented Self (*al-nafs al-muṭmaʾinna*).

The Contented Self (*al-Nafs al-Muṭmaʾinna*)	Details
Its journey (*safr*)...	is with Allah ﷻ (*maʿa Allāh*)
Its realm (*ʿālam*)...	is the celestial realm (*malak*)
Its locus (*maḥal*)...	is the inner secret (*sirr*)
Its state (*ḥāl*)...	is of union (*waṣal*)
Its inrush (*wārid*)...	is the *ṭarīqa*
Its light (*nūr*)...	is white

6.5 The Pleasing Self (al-Nafs al-Rāḍiya)

This is the fifth level of the lower self (*nafs*). Some *Shaykhs* and Sufis do not mention any separate level of the lower self (*nafs*) after the Contented Self (*al-nafs al-muṭmaʾinna*). In their view, the Pleasing Self (*al-nafs al-rāḍiya*), the Pleased Self (*al-nafs al-marḍiyya*) and the Perfect Self (*al-nafs al-kāmila* [*al-ṣāfiya*]) are higher stages and characteristics within the Contented Self (*al-nafs al-muṭmaʾinna*).

However, since the state of the lower self (*nafs*), its characteristics, stations, conditions and peculiarities keep changing, just like in the previous levels of the lower self (*nafs*), they should be counted as independent levels of the lower self (*nafs*) separate from the Contented Self (*al-nafs al-muṭmaʾinna*). Nevertheless, some Sufis are of the view that, rather than different types or levels of the lower self (*nafs*), there is only one lower self (*nafs*) because the Commanding Self (*al-nafs al-ammāra*), the Condemning Self (*al-nafs al-lawwāma*) and the Contented Self (*al-nafs al-muṭmaʾinna*) are all good and bad states of a single lower self (*nafs*).

Whether it is accepted that there is one lower self (*nafs*) or different levels of the lower self (*nafs*), it is inconsequential, as it boils down to the same thing. The difference is only in the expression. Even if they are considered to be the various conditions of the lower self (*nafs*), even then its attributes and states have changed, and the lower self (*nafs*) is not like before. Thus, the grades and ranks of those who possess it differ from their former state.

Those Sufis who consider there to be different levels of the lower self (*nafs*), their view is well constructed and easier to understand. However, this should not really be a point of contention. Whether these seven names are considered to be types, levels or attributes of the lower self (*nafs*) is immaterial.

After the above discussion on the categorisation of the lower self (*nafs*), the Pleasing Self (*al-nafs al-rāḍiya*) will be discussed. In this level of the lower self (*nafs*), a disposition comes into being that is pleased with the decisions and commandments of Allah ﷻ. Apparent circumstances may be positive or negative and there may even be pain or loss, but this type of the lower self (*nafs*) not only accepts it, considering it to be the will of Allah ﷻ, but maintains the state of inner contentment. Due to it being pleased with Allah ﷻ in all circumstances, it is named the 'Pleasing Self' (*al-nafs al-rāḍiya*).

It is mentioned in the Holy Qur'ān:

﴿ٱرْجِعِىٓ إِلَىٰ رَبِّكِ رَاضِيَةً مَّرْضِيَّةً﴾

Return to your Lord in such a state that you are both the aspirant to, and the aspired of, His pleasure (i.e., you seek His pleasure, and He seeks yours).[164]

The word is also mentioned when Prophet Zakariyyā ﷺ supplicated to Allah ﷻ for the son he wanted:

﴿يَرِثُنِى وَيَرِثُ مِنْ ءَالِ يَعْقُوبَ ۖ وَٱجْعَلْهُ رَبِّ رَضِيًّا﴾

(The one) who should be my heir (of divine blessing), and also the heir of (the chain of Prophethood from) the Children of Yaʿqūb (Jacob). And, O my Lord, (also) make him a recipient of Your Pleasure.'[165]

164 Qur'ān 89:27-28.

165 Qur'ān 19:6.

6.5.1 THE CHARACTERISTICS OF THE PLEASING SELF

The prevalent attributes of the Pleasing Self (*al-nafs al-rāḍiya*) are:

- Remembrance of Allah (*dhikr*) and contemplation (*fikr*)
- Asceticism (*zuhd*) and abstinence (*waraʿ*)
- Worship and inner struggle
- Vigilance of the commands of Allah (*taqwā*)
- Extreme love for Allah ﷻ
- Renunciation of everything other than Allah ﷻ
- Loyalty
- Miracles

6.5.2 THE METAPHORICAL FORMS OF THE PLEASING SELF IN DREAMS

The metaphorical forms seen in dreams that are evidence of the 'Pleasing Self' (*al-nafs al-rāḍiya*) include:

- Angels
- Heavenly brides
- Paradise
- Burrāq (a horse-like creature made out of light that travels at multiple speeds of light).
- The young male servants (*ghilmān*) of Paradise
- Jewellery
- Dress from Paradise
- The sun and the moon

6.5.3 INTERPRETATION OF THE METAPHORICAL FORMS

The following are some interpretations of the metaphorical forms seen in dreams:

- Seeing angels, Paradise, heavenly brides or the *ghilmān* is evidence of perfect intellect and nearness to Allah ﷻ.
- Seeing the sun and the moon represents the good news of divine gnosis (*maʿrifa*) being granted in the future.

6.5.4 Effective Invocations for the Pleasing Self – The Fifth Litany (Waẓīfa)

The effective invocation (*dhikr*) for this level of the lower self (*nafs*) is of the divine name *'al-Ḥayy'* (the Living). It is to be performed 500,000 times. This should be performed by repeating:

يَا حَيُّ أَنْتَ الْحَيُّ.

O the Ever-Living! You are the Ever-Living!

The following three focus invocations should be used. The first is:

يَا جَمِيلُ أَنْتَ الْحَيُّ.

O the Most Beautiful! You are the Ever-Living!

The second is:

يَا عَظِيمُ أَنْتَ الْحَيُّ.

O the Magnificent! You are the Ever-Living!

The third is:

يَا عَلِيُّ أَنْتَ الْحَيُّ.

O the Most High! You are the Ever-Living!

6.5.5 Performing the Litany (Waẓīfa) in Seclusion

This litany should be performed only 30,000 times, if performed in seclusion.

6.5.6 Tabular Outline for the Pleasing Self

The following is a tabular outline for the Pleasing Self (*al-nafs al-rāḍiya*).

The Pleasing Self (*al-Nafs al-Rāḍiya*)	Details
Its journey (*safr*)...	is in Allah ﷻ (*fī Allāh*)
Its realm (*ʿālam*)...	is the angelic realm (*malakūt*)
Its locus (*maḥal*)...	is the secret of the inner secret (*sirr al-sirr*)
Its state (*ḥāl*)...	is of annihilation (*fanāʾ*)
Its inrush (*wārid*)...	is the divine gnosis (*maʿrifa*)
Its light (*nūr*)...	is green

When the Pleasing Self (*al-nafs al-rāḍiya*) is mastered, then the station (*maqām*) known as 'Annihilation in God' (*fanāʾ fī Allāh*) will be acquired.

6.6 The Pleased Self (al-Nafs al-Marḍiyya)

This is the sixth and most perfect stage of the lower self (*nafs*). When the lower self (*nafs*) continues to be pleased with Allah ﷻ in every circumstance, and there is no wavering or faltering in its station, then this steadfastness (*istiqāma*) takes it to the stage of the 'Pleased Self' (*al-nafs al-marḍiyya*). This means Allah ﷻ is so pleased with that person that whatever His servant wishes will be granted. The reality is that a person's lower self (*nafs*) can only have the ability to be pleased with Allah ﷻ when Allah ﷻ Himself is pleased with him. The lower self (*nafs*) being pleased with Allah ﷻ is known as the station of the 'Pleasing' (*rāḍiya*) whereas Allah ﷻ being pleased with the lower self (*nafs*) is known as the station of the 'Pleased' (*marḍiyya*). They are both reciprocal to each other.

The station of the 'Pleased' (*marḍiyya*) has been mentioned in the Holy Qur'ān in relation to the Companions participating in the Pledge of Pleasure (*bayʿa al-riḍwān*):

﴿لَّقَدْ رَضِيَ ٱللَّهُ عَنِ ٱلْمُؤْمِنِينَ إِذْ يُبَايِعُونَكَ تَحْتَ ٱلشَّجَرَةِ﴾

Surely, Allah was well pleased with the believers when they pledged allegiance to you under the tree (at al-Ḥudaybiya).[166]

166 Qur'ān 48:18.

In another place:

﴿رَّضِيَ ٱللَّهُ عَنۡهُمۡ وَرَضُواْ عَنۡهُۚ﴾

Allah is pleased with them, and they are pleased with Him.[167]

Here, both the stations of the 'Pleased' (*marḍiyya*) and the 'Pleasing' (*rāḍiya*) are mentioned.

In the following verse, where the Contented Self (*al-nafs al-muṭma'inna*) is mentioned, both have been mentioned and the 'Pleased Station' (*marḍiyya*) has been mentioned after the 'Pleasing Station' (*rāḍiya*):

﴿يَٰٓأَيَّتُهَا ٱلنَّفۡسُ ٱلۡمُطۡمَئِنَّةُ ٢٧ ٱرۡجِعِيٓ إِلَىٰ رَبِّكِ رَاضِيَةٗ مَّرۡضِيَّةٗ﴾

O contented (pleased) self! Return to your Lord in such a state that you are both the aspirant to, and the aspired of, His pleasure (i.e., you seek His pleasure, and He seeks yours).[168]

The Holy Qur'ān has mentioned Prophet Ismāʿīl's 'Pleased Station' (*marḍiyya*):

﴿وَكَانَ يَأۡمُرُ أَهۡلَهُۥ بِٱلصَّلَوٰةِ وَٱلزَّكَوٰةِ وَكَانَ عِندَ رَبِّهِۦ مَرۡضِيّٗا﴾

And he used to enjoin on his family Prayer and Zakāh (the Alms-due), and (held) the station of marḍiyya in the presence of his Lord (i.e., his Lord was well-pleased with him).[169]

6.6.1 The Characteristics of the Pleased Self

The prevalent attributes of the Pleased Self (*al-nafs al-marḍiyya*) are:

- Gentleness and generosity
- Kindness and good morals
- Nearness to Allah ﷻ

---

167 Qur'ān 98:8.

168 Qur'ān 89:27-28.

169 Qur'ān 19:55.

- Obedience and compliance to the teachings of the Holy Prophet Muhammad ﷺ

It should be kept in mind that the virtuous attributes and states that were gained in the earlier levels of the lower self (*nafs*) gain greater permanence and progress further in the current level of the lower self (*nafs*).

6.6.2 The Metaphorical Forms of the Pleased Self in Dreams

The metaphorical forms seen in dreams that are evidence of the 'Pleased Self' (*al-nafs al-marḍiyya*) include:

- The seven heavens
- The sun
- The moon
- A star
- Lightning
- Thunder
- Fire
- A burning candle
- A bright lamp

6.6.3 Interpretation of the Metaphorical Forms

The following are some interpretations of the metaphorical forms seen in dreams:

- Seeing the heavens in a dream indicates one's vision being permanently connected to Allah ﷻ.
- Seeing a star represents the light of one's own lower self (*nafs*).
- Seeing fire is an indication towards one's lower self (*nafs*) being annihilated (*fanāʾ*).
- Seeing the moon represents the light of one's spiritual heart (*qalb*).
- Seeing the sun refers to the light of the spirit (*rūḥ*).
- Seeing or hearing lightning or thunder refers to one reconnecting to the correct path after being warned of committing negligence.

- The light from a candle or lamp represents light in the spiritual heart (*qalb*).

6.6.4 Effective Invocations for the Pleased Self – The Sixth Litany (Waẓīfa)

The effective invocation (*dhikr*) for this level of the lower self (*nafs*) is of the divine name *'al-Qayyūm'* (the Sustainer of All). It is to be performed 500,000 times. This should be performed by repeating:

يَا قَيُّومُ.

O the Sustainer of All!

The following three focus invocations should be used. The first is:

يَا قَيُّومُ يَا كَافِي.

O Sustainer of All! O Sufficient!

The second is:

يَا قَيُّومُ يَا مُغْنِي.

O Sustainer of All! O Enricher!

The third is:

يَا قَيُّومُ يَا قَادِرُ.

O Sustainer of All! O All-Powerful!

6.6.5 Performing the Litany (Waẓīfa) in Seclusion

This litany should be performed only 20,000 times, if performed in seclusion.

6.6.6 Tabular Outline for the Pleased Self

The following is a tabular outline for the Pleased Self (*al-nafs al-marḍiyya*).

The Pleased Self (*al-Nafs al-Marḍiyya*)	Details
Its journey (*safr*)...	is from Allah ﷻ (*ʿan Allāh*)
Its realm (*ʿālam*)...	is the realm of the powerful (*jabarūt*)
Its locus (*maḥal*)...	is the hidden secret (*khafī*)
Its state (*ḥāl*)...	is of amazement
Its inrush (*wārid*)...	is the ultimate reality (*ḥaqīqa*)
Its light (*nūr*)...	is black

6.7 The Perfect Self (al-Nafs al-Kāmila [al-Ṣāfiya])

This is the seventh self (*nafs*) and the final station of perfection. The following verses refer to this station:

﴿يَـٰٓأَيَّتُهَا ٱلنَّفْسُ ٱلْمُطْمَئِنَّةُ ﴿٢٧﴾ ٱرْجِعِىٓ إِلَىٰ رَبِّكِ رَاضِيَةً مَّرْضِيَّةً ﴿٢٨﴾
فَٱدْخُلِى فِى عِبَـٰدِى ﴿٢٩﴾ وَٱدْخُلِى جَنَّتِى﴾

O contented (pleased) self! Return to your Lord in such a state that you are both the aspirant to, and the aspired of, His pleasure (i.e., you seek His pleasure, and He seeks yours). So join My (perfect) servants. And enter My Paradise (of nearness and sight). So join My (perfect) servants. And enter My Paradise (of nearness and sight).[170]

In this verse, the command to the lower self (*nafs*) to '*join My (perfect) servants*' is raising the rank of the lower self (*nafs*) to perfection (*kāmiliyya*). The words '*enter My Paradise*' is also bestowing it the higher station. Ghawth al-Aʿẓam Shaykh ʿAbd al-Qādir al-Jīlānī mentions that there are a few types and levels of Paradise. They are explained below.

I. The Eternal Paradise (Janna al-Maʾwā)

This is the Paradise in the celestial realm. When the lower self (*nafs*) returns to Allah ﷻ and has travelled through the path of the Sharia, then it reaches this Paradise, the station of which is near the Farthest

170 Qur'ān 89:27-30.

Lote Tree (*Sidra al-Muntahā*).

Allah Almighty states:

﴿وَلَقَدْ رَءَاهُ نَزْلَةً أُخْرَىٰ ۝١٣ عِندَ سِدْرَةِ ٱلْمُنتَهَىٰ ۝١٤ عِندَهَا جَنَّةُ ٱلْمَأْوَىٰٓ﴾

And assuredly, he saw Him (Allah Unveiled) the second time (again and you argue only about seeing Him once). At the farthest Lote-Tree (Sidra al-Muntahā). Adjacent to that is the Eternal Paradise (Janna al-Maʾwā).[171]

II. The Paradise of Bliss (Janna al-Naʿīm)

This is the Paradise in the angelic realm. The lower self (*nafs*) attains this upon successfully traversing the spiritual path (*ṭarīqa*). This is known as the 'Station of the Righteous' (*maqām al-abrār*), which is mentioned in the Holy Qurʾān:

﴿إِنَّ ٱلْأَبْرَارَ لَفِى نَعِيمٍ ۝٢٢ عَلَى ٱلْأَرَآئِكِ يَنظُرُونَ ۝٢٣ تَعْرِفُ فِى وُجُوهِهِمْ نَضْرَةَ ٱلنَّعِيمِ ۝٢٤ يُسْقَوْنَ مِن رَّحِيقٍ مَّخْتُومٍ ۝٢٥ خِتَٰمُهُۥ مِسْكٌ ۚ وَفِى ذَٰلِكَ فَلْيَتَنَافَسِ ٱلْمُتَنَٰفِسُونَ﴾

Indeed, the truly pious, (joyful and glad,) will be in blissful Paradise, reclining on couches, enjoying the wonderful sights. You will find on their faces the glow and freshness of bliss and delight. They shall be served with securely sealed delicious and holy beverage. Its seal will be musk. And (it is this beverage which) all aspirants should hastily strive and compete to acquire. (Some seek the drink of bliss whilst others long for the drink of nearness, and still others yearn for the drink of countenance—all will be served according to their respective tastes).[172]

Likewise, it is also stated:

---

[171] Qur'ān 53:13-15.

[172] Qur'ān 83:22-26.

﴿إِنَّ ٱلۡأَبۡرَارَ يَشۡرَبُونَ مِن كَأۡسٖ كَانَ مِزَاجُهَا كَافُورًا ٥ عَيۡنٗا
يَشۡرَبُ بِهَا عِبَادُ ٱللَّهِ يُفَجِّرُونَهَا تَفۡجِيرٗا ٦ يُوفُونَ بِٱلنَّذۡرِ
وَيَخَافُونَ يَوۡمٗا كَانَ شَرُّهُۥ مُسۡتَطِيرٗا ٧ وَيُطۡعِمُونَ ٱلطَّعَامَ عَلَىٰ
حُبِّهِۦ مِسۡكِينٗا وَيَتِيمٗا وَأَسِيرًا ٨ إِنَّمَا نُطۡعِمُكُمۡ لِوَجۡهِ ٱللَّهِ لَا
نُرِيدُ مِنكُمۡ جَزَآءٗ وَلَا شُكُورًا ٩ إِنَّا نَخَافُ مِن رَّبِّنَا يَوۡمًا
عَبُوسٗا قَمۡطَرِيرٗا ١٠ فَوَقَىٰهُمُ ٱللَّهُ شَرَّ ذَٰلِكَ ٱلۡيَوۡمِ وَلَقَّىٰهُمۡ نَضۡرَةٗ
وَسُرُورٗا ١١ وَجَزَىٰهُم بِمَا صَبَرُواْ جَنَّةٗ وَحَرِيرٗا ١٢ مُّتَّكِـِٔينَ فِيهَا
عَلَى ٱلۡأَرَآئِكِۖ لَا يَرَوۡنَ فِيهَا شَمۡسٗا وَلَا زَمۡهَرِيرٗا ١٣ وَدَانِيَةً
عَلَيۡهِمۡ ظِلَٰلُهَا وَذُلِّلَتۡ قُطُوفُهَا تَذۡلِيلٗا ١٤ وَيُطَافُ عَلَيۡهِم بِـَٔانِيَةٖ
مِّن فِضَّةٖ وَأَكۡوَابٖ كَانَتۡ قَوَارِيرَا۠ ١٥ قَوَارِيرَاْ مِن فِضَّةٖ قَدَّرُوهَا
تَقۡدِيرٗا ١٦ وَيُسۡقَوۡنَ فِيهَا كَأۡسٗا كَانَ مِزَاجُهَا زَنجَبِيلًا ١٧ عَيۡنٗا
فِيهَا تُسَمَّىٰ سَلۡسَبِيلٗا ١٨ وَيَطُوفُ عَلَيۡهِمۡ وِلۡدَٰنٞ مُّخَلَّدُونَ إِذَا
رَأَيۡتَهُمۡ حَسِبۡتَهُمۡ لُؤۡلُؤٗا مَّنثُورٗا ١٩ وَإِذَا رَأَيۡتَ ثَمَّ رَأَيۡتَ نَعِيمٗا
وَمُلۡكٗا كَبِيرًا ٢٠ عَٰلِيَهُمۡ ثِيَابُ سُندُسٍ خُضۡرٞ وَإِسۡتَبۡرَقٞۖ وَحُلُّوٓاْ
أَسَاوِرَ مِن فِضَّةٖ وَسَقَىٰهُمۡ رَبُّهُمۡ شَرَابٗا طَهُورًا ٢١ إِنَّ هَٰذَا كَانَ
لَكُمۡ جَزَآءٗ وَكَانَ سَعۡيُكُم مَّشۡكُورًا﴾

Surely, the sincerely devoted and obedient will drink from the cups (of the holy drink) mixed with kāfūr (to enhance its aroma, colour and taste). (Kāfūr is) a spring (in Paradise) that (the privileged) servants of Allah (i.e., the Awliyāʾ Allāh) will drink from, and will (also) make it flow to wherever they will desire in the form of small brooks (to make others drink of it). (These privileged servants of Allah are those) who fulfil their vows and keep fearing that Day whose severity spreads afar. And they give (their own) food, in deep love of Allah, to the needy, the orphan and prisoner (out of sacrifice, despite their own desire and need for it), (And say:) 'We are feeding you only to please Allah. We do not seek any recompense from you nor (wish for) any thanks. We fear from our Lord the Day which will make (the faces) look very dark (and) ugly.' So Allah will save them from the terror of that Day (for their fear of Allah) and will grant them freshness, bloom and blush (on their faces) and ecstasy and delight (in their hearts), and will bless them with Gardens (to live in) and silky clothes (to wear), a reward for their patience. Reclining in it against cushions on raised couches, they will find there neither intense cold nor heat. And the shades (of trees in Paradise) will close upon them, and the bunches of their (fruits) will be hanging low. And (the servants) will go round them with vessels of silver and (pure and clean) goblets of shining glass, and glasses made of silver which they will have filled with exact measures (according to everyone's desire). And they will be made to drink there cups of (the holy drink) mixed with Zanjabīl. (Zanjabīl is) a spring in this (Paradise) named Salsabīl. And going round them will be (innocent) adolescents who will remain ever-young. When you will see them, you will consider them as scattered pearls. And when you will look (at Paradise), you will find blessings (in abundance) and a mighty kingdom (all around). They will be clad in green, fine silk and rich brocade attire, and they will be made to wear silver bracelets, and their Lord will make them drink a holy beverage. Surely, that will be your reward and your hard work is acknowledged.[173]

III. THE GARDEN OF PARADISE (JANNA AL-FIRDAWS)

This is the Paradise (*Janna*) in the Realm of Divine Power (*ʿālam al-jabarūt*). This is only available to the lower self (*nafs*) after completing the journey of divine gnosis (*maʿrifa*). Allah ﷻ states regarding it:

﴿إِنَّ ٱلَّذِينَ ءَامَنُوا۟ وَعَمِلُوا۟ ٱلصَّٰلِحَٰتِ كَانَتْ لَهُمْ جَنَّٰتُ ٱلْفِرْدَوْسِ نُزُلًا ۝١٠٧ خَٰلِدِينَ فِيهَا لَا يَبْغُونَ عَنْهَا حِوَلًا﴾

[173] Qur'ān 76:5-22.

> *Surely, those who believe and do good deeds persistently shall have the Gardens of Paradise as their hospitality. They will always live there. They will never seek any change (of abode) from there.*[174]

This is where the pure selves (*nufūs*) will enjoy the hospitality of the Divine. The host is the Most Forgiving, the Most Merciful and the Most Generous Lord Himself. Allah ﷻ states in this regard:

﴿إِنَّ ٱلَّذِينَ قَالُوا۟ رَبُّنَا ٱللَّهُ ثُمَّ ٱسْتَقَـٰمُوا۟ تَتَنَزَّلُ عَلَيْهِمُ ٱلْمَلَـٰٓئِكَةُ
أَلَّا تَخَافُوا۟ وَلَا تَحْزَنُوا۟ وَأَبْشِرُوا۟ بِٱلْجَنَّةِ ٱلَّتِى كُنتُمْ تُوعَدُونَ ﴿٣٠﴾
نَحْنُ أَوْلِيَآؤُكُمْ فِى ٱلْحَيَوٰةِ ٱلدُّنْيَا وَفِى ٱلْـَٔاخِرَةِ ۖ وَلَكُمْ فِيهَا مَا
تَشْتَهِىٓ أَنفُسُكُمْ وَلَكُمْ فِيهَا مَا تَدَّعُونَ ﴿٣١﴾ نُزُلًا مِّنْ غَفُورٍ
رَّحِيمٍ﴾

> *Surely, those who say: 'Our Lord is Allah,' then stick to it (firmly), angels descend upon them (and say:) 'Do not fear or grieve and rejoice in the Paradise that you were promised. We are your friends and helpers in the life of this world and in the Hereafter (too). And there is for you every blessing that you long for. And all those things that you ask for are (available) for you there. (This) is hospitality from the Most Forgiving, Ever-Merciful (Lord).'*[175]

The beautiful qualities of the people who will be entered into the Garden of Paradise (*Janna al-Firdaws*) are mentioned in the Holy Qur'ān in the following words:

﴿قَدْ أَفْلَحَ ٱلْمُؤْمِنُونَ ﴿١﴾ ٱلَّذِينَ هُمْ فِى صَلَاتِهِمْ خَـٰشِعُونَ ﴿٢﴾
وَٱلَّذِينَ هُمْ عَنِ ٱللَّغْوِ مُعْرِضُونَ ﴿٣﴾ وَٱلَّذِينَ هُمْ لِلزَّكَوٰةِ فَـٰعِلُونَ ﴿٤﴾
وَٱلَّذِينَ هُمْ لِفُرُوجِهِمْ حَـٰفِظُونَ ﴿٥﴾ إِلَّا عَلَىٰٓ أَزْوَٰجِهِمْ أَوْ مَا مَلَكَتْ
أَيْمَـٰنُهُمْ فَإِنَّهُمْ غَيْرُ مَلُومِينَ ﴿٦﴾ فَمَنِ ٱبْتَغَىٰ وَرَآءَ ذَٰلِكَ فَأُو۟لَـٰٓئِكَ

174 Qur'ān 18:107-108.

175 Qur'ān 41:30-33.

هُمُ ٱلْعَادُونَ ۞ وَٱلَّذِينَ هُمْ لِأَمَٰنَٰتِهِمْ وَعَهْدِهِمْ رَٰعُونَ ۞ وَٱلَّذِينَ
هُمْ عَلَىٰ صَلَوَٰتِهِمْ يُحَافِظُونَ ۞ أُوْلَٰٓئِكَ هُمُ ٱلْوَٰرِثُونَ ۞ ٱلَّذِينَ
يَرِثُونَ ٱلْفِرْدَوْسَ هُمْ فِيهَا خَٰلِدُونَ﴾

Certainly, the believers have attained their goal; those who become most humble and submissive in their Prayers, and who (always) keep away from absurd talk, and who (always) pay Zakah (the Alms-due [and keep purifying their wealth and souls]), and who guard their private parts (all the time), except from their wives or those slave-girls who are the possessions of their hands. (If they go to them according to the Islamic injunctions,) there is surely no blame on them. But whoever desires someone beyond these (lawful women), it is they who are transgressors (and disobedient). And those who are watchful of their trusts and their pledges, and who guard their Prayers (with persistence), it is they who will be the inheritors (of Paradise). They will (also) inherit the most superior Gardens of Paradise (where all the bounties, comforts and pleasures of nearness to Allah will abound). They will live there forever.[176]

IV. The Paradise of Nearness (Janna al-Qurba)

This is the highest of all the Paradises and is in the Realm of Divinity (*ʿālam al-lāhūt*). The lower self (*nafs*) attains this upon completing the journey of reality (*ḥaqīqa*). This is only available to those who have been bestowed divine nearness (i.e. the *muqarrabīn*). The worshipful servants (*ʿābidīn*) and ascetics (*zāhidīn*) travel from the world to Paradise, whereas the Gnostics (*ʿārifīn*) and divine lovers (*ʿāshiqīn*) travel from Paradise to divine nearness (*qurba*).

The following Qur'ānic verses refer to this station:

﴿وَمِزَاجُهُۥ مِن تَسْنِيمٍ ۞ عَيْنًا يَشْرَبُ بِهَا ٱلْمُقَرَّبُونَ﴾

And this (beverage of Paradise) will be mixed with the water of Tasnīm. (This Tasnīm) is a fountain at which only those drawn

176 Qur'ān 23:1-11.

close will drink.[177]

Those who are fortunate to drink from this fountain know best whether it is a fountain of nearness or an eye of love and if it is drunk from glasses or through the eyes because this is the station of:

﴿وَلَكُمْ فِيهَا مَا تَشْتَهِي أَنفُسُكُمْ﴾

And there is for you every blessing that you long for.[178]

Those who reach this station do not desire anything from the bounties of Paradise. They only desire the vision of the Beloved ﷻ repeatedly, thus they are granted it every time.

In *Sūra al-Wāqiʿa*, Allah ﷻ has stated that in the Hereafter, people will be divided into three categories:

1. The People of the Left Hand (*Aṣḥāb al-Mashʾama* or *Aṣḥāb al-Shimāl*): These are the people who will enter the various levels of Hell according to their states and deeds.
2. The People of the Right Hand (*Aṣḥāb al-Maymana* or *Aṣḥāb al-Yamīn*): These are the people who will enter Paradise. They will also enter the various levels of Paradise according to their states and deeds. As mentioned earlier, they will enter either the Eternal Paradise (*Janna al-Maʾwā*), the Paradise of Bliss (*Janna al-Naʿīm*) or the Garden of Paradise (*Janna al-Firdaws*).
3. Those Drawn Near to Allah ﷻ (*al-Muqarribūn*): The people of divine nearness (*qurba*) will also attain the aforementioned levels of Paradise (*Janna*). In addition to this, they will achieve the very highest and reserved level known as the Station of Proximity (*maqām al-qurba*).

   For those who are drawn near, Paradise will be their place of dwelling and the Station of Proximity will be their place of recreation. They will live in Paradise, and the Blissful Paradise (*Janna al-Naʿīm*) and the Garden of Paradise (*Janna al-Firdaws*) will be their residence. But they will roam freely in the Paradise

177 Qur'ān 83:27-28.

178 Qur'ān 41:33.

of Nearness (*Janna al-Qurba*) and the Station of Proximity (*maqām al-qurba*) will be their place of comfort.

In Paradise, the beauty and glory of the Beloved ﷻ will be manifested from behind a veil, but in the Station of Proximity (*maqām al-qurba*), the Beloved's glory and beauty will be manifested unveiled. The Holy Qur'ān mentions three blessings for those at the Station of Proximity (*maqām al-qurba*):

﴿فَأَمَّآ إِن كَانَ مِنَ ٱلْمُقَرَّبِينَ فَرَوْحٌ وَرَيْحَانٌ وَجَنَّتُ نَعِيمٍ﴾

Then if he (who died) was of those drawn near, for him is Paradise packed with bounties, pleasure and delight and spiritual sustenance and comforts.[179]

The people of nearness (*qurba*) will simultaneously receive the three blessings of '*rawḥ*' (comfort), '*rayḥān*' (most beautiful delights) and *Janna al-Naʿīm* (the Blissful Paradise). The reality is that when Allah ﷻ said, '*and enter my Paradise*', it actually refers to the Station of Proximity and Comfort (*maqām al-qurba wa al-rāḥa*).

6.7.1 THE CHARACTERISTICS OF THE PERFECT SELF

The prevalent attributes of the Perfect Self (*al-nafs al-kāmila* [*al-ṣāfiya*]) are:

- Seclusion
- Worship
- Separation from other than Allah ﷻ
- Silence
- Truthfulness
- Helping and assisting
- Fulfilling promises
- Obedience to Allah ﷻ
- Having perfection in both the Affinity of Servanthood (*nisba al-ʿabdiyya*) and the Muhammadan Affinity (*nisba al-Muḥammadiyya*)

179 Qur'ān 56:88-89.

6.7.2 THE METAPHORICAL FORMS OF THE PERFECT SELF IN DREAMS

The metaphorical forms seen in dreams that are evidence of the 'Perfect Self' (*al-nafs al-kāmila* [*al-ṣāfiya*]) include:

- Rain
- Snow and hail
- Streams
- Rivers
- Springs
- Wells

6.7.3 INTERPRETATION OF THE METAPHORICAL FORMS

All of these metaphorical forms are the signs of the opening of the path to Allah ﷻ. Allah Almighty states in the Holy Qur'ān:

﴿وَٱلَّذِينَ جَٰهَدُوا۟ فِينَا لَنَهْدِيَنَّهُمْ سُبُلَنَا﴾

As for those who strive in our way, we open all our ways to them.[180]

Rain in particular refers to mercy, while snow and hail refer to the abundance of mercy. Streams, rivers and wells refer to divine gnosis (*maʿrifa*) and the attainment of sincerity (*ikhlāṣ*).

6.7.4 EFFECTIVE INVOCATIONS FOR THE PERFECT SELF – THE SEVENTH LITANY (WAẒĪFA)

The effective invocation (*dhikr*) for this level of the lower self (*nafs*) is of the divine name '*al-Qahhār*' (the Dominant Over All). It is to be performed 500,000 times. This should be performed by repeating:

يَا قَهَّارُ.

O Dominant Over All!

The following three focus invocations should be used. The first is:

---

[180] Qur'ān 29:69.

يَا قَيُّومُ يَا قَهَّارُ.

O Sustainer of All! O Dominant Over All!

The second is:

يَا جَبَّارُ يَا قَهَّارُ.

O Compeller! O Dominant Over All!

The third is:

يَا وَدُودُ يَا قَهَّارُ.

O Most Loving! O Dominant Over All!

6.7.5 Performing the Litany (Waẓīfa) in Seclusion

This litany should be performed only 10,000 times, if performed in seclusion.

6.7.6 Tabular Outline for the Perfect Self

The following is a tabular outline for the Perfect Self (*al-nafs al-kāmila* [*al-ṣāfiya*]).

The Perfect Self (*al-Nafs al-Kāmila*)	Details
Its journey (*safr*)...	is with Allah ﷻ (*biʾLlāh*)
Its realm (*ʿālam*)...	is Divinity (*lāhūt*)
Its locus (*maḥal*)...	is the innermost secret (*akhfā*)
Its state (*ḥāl*)...	is of subsistence (*baqāʾ*)
Its inrush (*wārid*)...	is the Muhammadan reality (*Muḥammadiyya*)
Its light (*nūr*)...	is colourless

IMPORTANT NOTE: The seeker (*sālik*) must complete these seven litanies. All seven litanies constitute one set. Upon completing all seven litanies, they should all be done again for the second set. By repeating this process all over again, seven sets have to be completed. After completing the seventh set, Allah ﷻ, out of His Mercy for the seeker, will open the paths towards Him.

6.8 The Perfect Self (al-Nafs al-Kāmila), the Muhammadan Station (Maqām al-Muḥammadiyya) and the Court of Divine Majesty (Ḥaḍra al-Ulūhiyya)

When the Pleased Self (*al-nafs al-marḍiyya*) completes the inrush journey of knowledge and awareness about Reality (*ḥaqīqa*), then it completes the grades of the realm of the powerful (*jabarūt*). Upon reaching the very end, a call is given:

﴿فَٱدۡخُلِي فِي عِبَٰدِي﴾

Enter amongst My servants.[181]

So, the Pleased Self (*al-nafs al-marḍiyya*) is entered into the realm of divinity (*ʿālam al-lāhūt*) where it is placed in special nearness (*qurba khāṣṣa*). This is the station of perfection (*maqām al-kamāl*) where all the veils are lifted. Here the seeker (*sālik*) reaches the oceans of the Muhammadan Infusion (*al-wurūd al-Muḥammadiyya*).

The Muhammadan Infusion (*al-wurūd al-Muḥammadiyya*) is more advanced than the milestones of the Sharia, the stations of the *ṭarīqa*, the grades of divine gnosis (*maʿrifa*) and the levels of reality (*ḥaqīqa*). Beyond it is the station known as the 'Muhammadan Reality' (*al-ḥaqīqa al-Muḥammadiyya*), which is hidden within one thousand veils of light. Sulṭān al-ʿĀrifīn Bāyazīd Bustāmī says about them:

غُصْتُ لُجَّةَ الْمَعَارِفِ طَالِبًا لِلْوُقُوفِ عَلَى عَيْنِ حَقِيقَةِ النَّبِيِّ ﷺ، فَإِذَا بَيْنِي وَبَيْنَهَا أَلْفُ حِجَابٍ مِنْ نُورٍ، لَوْ دَنَوْتُ مِنَ الْحِجَابِ الْأَوَّلِ لَاحْتَرَقْتُ بِهِ كَمَا تَحْتَرِقُ الشَّعْرَةُ إِذَا أُلْقِيَتْ فِي النَّارِ.

In order to understand the Reality of the Prophet (*al-ḥaqīqa al-Muḥammadiyya* ﷺ), I intended to head towards the first

[181] Qur'ān 89:29.

> veil out of the one thousand veils of light that encircle the Muhammadan Reality (*al-ḥaqīqa al-Muḥammadiyya*) and I was told that if I even approached the first veil I would be burnt to ashes![182]

At this point, the spiritual flight of a human being comes to an end. It is the doorstep to the court of the Holy Prophet Muhammad ﷺ. This is the highest point that sainthood can reach to. The Holy Prophet ﷺ himself appears at each grade according to its stations and capabilities. These are the courts where the attendees are in the direct presence of the Holy Prophet ﷺ.

As far as the Muhammadan Reality (*al-ḥaqīqa al-Muḥammadiyya*) is concerned, nobody has access to it. Even Angel Jibrīl ﷺ cannot go there. Above this is the Court of Divine Majesty (*ḥaḍra al-ulūhiyya*). The Muhammadan Reality (*al-ḥaqīqa al-Muḥammadiyya*) is a rationally possible reality whereas the divine majesty is a rationally necessary reality. The former is the reality of servitude while the latter is the reality of Lordship.

The union of these two realities is completely unknown, even the angels, who are most informed on divine matters, are not permitted beyond the Farthest Lote Tree (*sidra al-muntaḥā*). The meeting of these two realities sometimes takes place in the shape of '*danā fa-tadallā*'[183] (He (the Lord of Honour) drew closer (to His Beloved Muhammad ﷺ) and then drew even closer), or sometimes in the shape of '*qāba qawsayn aw adnā*'[184] (a distance measuring only two bow-lengths or even less). After the revelation of these words, thinking or commenting further upon this has been prohibited.

When the complete awareness of the Muhammadan Reality (*al-ḥaqīqa al-Muḥammadiyya*) cannot be perceived, then having complete awareness of the Court of Divine Majesty (*ḥaḍra al-ulūhiyya*) is impossible. The Holy Prophet ﷺ himself stated:

أَفَلَا أَكُونُ عَبْدًا شَكُورًا.

---

182 Yūsuf b. Ismāʿīl al-Nabhānī, *Jawāhir al-Bihār*, 3:67.

183 Qur'ān 53:8.

184 Qur'ān 53:9.

Should I not be a grateful servant.[185]

Then, on the other side, after bestowing upon the Holy Prophet ﷺ the highest level of the Station of Divine Belovedness and Nearness (*maḥbūbiyya wa muqarrabiyya*), Allah ﷻ stated:

﴿فَأَوْحَىٰٓ إِلَىٰ عَبْدِهِۦ مَآ أَوْحَىٰ﴾

So (on that station of nearness,) He (Allah) revealed to His (Beloved) servant whatever He revealed.[186]

Upon bestowing His beloved servant ﷺ the station of nearness (*aw adnā*), He revealed to him whatever He revealed. These words are telling of two secrets. The first is that the station of the Muhammadan Reality (*al-ḥaqīqa al-Muḥammadiyya*) even after going beyond all possible grades of proximity is still servanthood (*ʿabdiyya*). Secondly, that gaining awareness of the nature of the mutual relationship between the Muhammadan Reality (*al-ḥaqīqa al-Muḥammadiyya*) and the Court of the Divine Majesty (*ḥaḍra al-ulūhiyya*) is not possible because Allah ﷻ, by saying '*He revealed whatever He revealed*,' has decided to keep it as the greatest secret. Only the Almighty ﷻ and His beloved ﷺ know.

The end point of the spiritual journey is at the doorstep of the Muhammadan Reality (*al-ḥaqīqa al-Muḥammadiyya*), and this is where our discourse on spiritual wayfaring ends.

---

185 Narrated by al-Bukhārī in *al-Ṣaḥīḥ*: *Kitāb al-Tahajjud* [The Book of the Night Vigil Prayer], chapter: 'The Prophet's standing in prayer until his feet become swollen', 1:380 §1078.

186 Qur'ān 53:10.

BIBLIOGRAPHY

al-Qur᾽ān

ʿAbd al-Qādir al-Jīlānī, Abū Ṣāliḥ Shaykh ʿAbd al-Qādir b. Mūsā b. ʿAbd Allāh al-Jīlānī. *Ghunya al-Ṭālibīn*. Beirut, Lebanon: Maktaba al-Thiqāfa, n.d.

—. *Sirr al-Asrār*. Lahore, Pakistan: Tufayl Art Press, 1401 AH.

—. *Futūḥ al-Ghayb*. Lahore, Pakistan: Publishing Company Lahore, 1998 CE.

—. *al-Fatḥ al-Rabbānī*. Beirut, Lebanon: Dār al-Fikr, 1st edition, n.d.

Abū Nuʿaym al-Aṣbahānī, Aḥmad b. ʿAbd Allāh b. Aḥmad b. Isḥāq b. Mūsā b. Mahrān al-Aṣbahānī. *Ḥilya al-Awliyā᾽ wa Ṭabaqāt al-Aṣfiyā᾽*. Beirut: Dār al-Kitāb al-ʿArabī, 1405 AH/1985 CE.

Abū Saʿd al-Nīsāpūrī, ʿAbd al-Malik b. Muḥammad Ibrāhīm al-Kharkūshī. *Tahdhīb al-Asrār*. Abu Dhabi: al-Majmaʿ al-Thiqāfī, 1999 CE.

Abū Yaʿlā, Aḥmad b. ʿAlī b. al-Muthannā b. Yaḥyā b. ʿĪsā b. Hilāl al-Mūṣilī al-Tamīmī. *al-Musnad*. Damascus, Syria: Dār al-Ma᾽mūn li al-Turāth, 1st edition 1404 AH/1984 CE.

Aḥmad al-Rifāʿī, Abū al-ʿAbbās al-Sayyid Aḥmad b. ʿAlī al-Ḥusaynī al-Rifāʿī. *al-Burhān al-Mu᾽ayyad*. Damascus, Syria: Maktaba al-Ḥalwānī, n.d.

ʿAlī al-Hujwayrī, Abū al-Ḥasan ʿAlī b. ʿUthmān b. Abī ʿAlī al-Jallābī al-Ghaznawī. *Kashf al-Maḥjūb*. Alexandria, Egypt: Maktaba al-Iskandariyya, 1394 AH/1974 CE.

ʿAynī, Badr al-Dīn Abū Muḥammad Maḥmūd b. Aḥmad b. Mūsā b. Aḥmad b. Ḥusayn b. Yūsuf b. Maḥmūd. *ʿUmda al-Qārī Sharḥ Ṣaḥīḥ al-Bukhārī*. Beirut, Lebanon: Dār al-Fikr, 1399 AH/1979 CE & Dār Iḥyāʾ al-Turāth al-ʿArabī, n.d.

Baghawī, Muḥyī al-Sunna Abū Muḥammad al-Ḥusayn b. Masʿūd, al-. *Maʿālim al-Tanzīl*. Dār Ṭayba, 1417 AH/1997 CE & Dār al-Maʿrifa, 1407 AH/1987 CE.

Bayḥaqī, Abū Bakr Aḥmad b. Ḥusayn b. ʿAlī b. ʿAbd Allāh b. Mūsā, al-. *Dalāʾil al-Nubuwwa*. Beirut: Dār al-Kutub al-ʿIlmiyya, 1405 AH/1985 CE.

—. *al-Sunan al-Kubrā*. Mecca: Maktaba Dār al-Bāz, 1414 AH/1994 CE.

—. *al-Madkhal ilā al-Sunan al-Kubrā*. Kuwait: al-Khulafāʾ li al-Kitāb al-Islāmī, 1404 AH & Cairo, Egypt: Dār al-Yusr li al-Nashr wa al-Tawzīʿ, n.d.

Bopālī, Nawāb Ṣiddīq Ḥasan Khān Qanūjī. *al-Rawḍ al-Khaṣīb*. Akbarabad, India: Maṭbaʿ Akbarabad, 1289 AH.

Bukhārī, Abū ʿAbd Allāh Muḥammad b. Ismāʾīl b. Ibrāhīm b. Mughīra. *al-Ṣaḥīḥ*. Beirut: Dār al-Qalam, 1401 AH/1981 CE.

—. *al-Adab al-Mufrad*. Beirut: Dār al-Bashāʾir al-Islāmiyya, 1409 AH/1989 CE.

Dhahabī, Shams al-Dīn Muḥammad b. Aḥmad b. ʿUthmān, al-. *Kitāb al-Zuhd wa al-Ḥikma*. Damascus, Syria: Dār al-Muqtabas, 1438 AH/2017 CE.

Fayrūzābādī, Majd al-Dīn Muḥammad b. Yaqʿūb, al-. *Safr al-Saʿāda*. Beirut, Lebanon: al-Maktaba al-ʿAṣriyya, 1416 AH/1995 CE.

Ghazālī, Ḥujja al-Islām Abū Ḥāmid Muḥammad, al-. *Iḥyāʾ ʿUlūm al-Dīn*. Egypt: Maṭbaʿa ʿUthmāniyya, 1352 AH/1933 CE.

Gongohī, Rashīd Aḥmad. *Imdād al-Sulūk*. Sheikhupura, Pakistan: Kutub Khāna Sharaf al-Rashīd, n.d.

Ḥalabī, ʿAlī b. Burhān al-Dīn. *al-Sīra al-Ḥalabiyya (Insān al-ʿUyūn fī Sīra al-Amīn al-Maʾmūn* ﷺ*)*. Beirut: Dār al-Maʿrifa, 1400 AH.

Ḥākim, Abū ʿAbd Allāh Muḥammad b. ʿAbd Allāh b. Muḥammad, al-. *al-Mustadrak ʿalā al-Ṣaḥīḥayn*. Beirut, Lebanon: Dār al-Kutub al-

ʿIlmiyya, 1st edition, 1411 AH/1990 CE & Makkah, Saudi Arabia: Dār al-Bāz li al-Nashr wa al-Tawzīʿ, n.d.

Ḥakīm al-Tirmidhī, Abū ʿAbd Allāh Muḥammad b. ʿAlī b. Ḥasan b. Bashīr. *Nawādir al-Uṣūl fī Aḥādīth al-Rasūl*. Beirut: Dār al-Jīl, 1992 CE.

Haythamī, Nūr al-Dīn Abū al-Ḥasan ʿAlī b. Abī Bakr b. Sulaymān, al-. *Majmaʿ al-Zawāʾid wa Manbaʿ al-Fawāʾid*. Cairo, Egypt: Dār al-Rayyān li al-Turāth & Beirut, Lebanon: Dār al-Kitāb al-ʿArabī, 1407 AH/1987 CE.

Hindī, ʿAlāʾ al-Dīn ʿAlī b. Ḥisām al-Dīn al-Muttaqī, al-. *Kanz al-ʿUmmā fī Sunan al-Aqwāl wa al-Afʾāl*. Beirut, Lebanon: Muʾassasa al-Risāla, 1399 AH/1979 CE & Dār al-Kutub al-ʿIlmiyya, 1419 AH.

Ibn Abī Bakr al-Rāzī, Muḥammad ʿAbd al-Qādir Shams al-Dīn. *Ḥadāʾiq al-Ḥaqāʾiq*. Cairo, Egypt: Maktaba al-Thiqāfa al-Dīniyya, 1422 AH/2002 CE.

Ibn Abī Shayba, Abū Bakr ʿAbd Allāh b. Muḥammad b. Ibrāhīm b. ʿUthmān. *al-Muṣannaf*. Riyadh, Saudi Arabia: Maktaba al-Rashīd, 1st edition, 1409 AH & Karachi, Pakistan: Idāra al-Qurʾān wa al-ʿUlūm, n.d.

Ibn ʿAjība, Abū al-ʿAbbās Aḥmad b. Muḥammad b. al-Mahdī b. al-Ḥusayn b. Muḥammad b. ʿAjība al-Idrīsī al-Ḥasanī al-Sharīf. *Īqāẓ al-Himam fī Sharḥ al-Ḥikam*. Qom, Iran: al-Murāsīlāt, n.d.

Ibn Hishām, Abu Muḥammad ʿAbd al-Malik Hishām al-Himyarī. *al-Sīra al-Nabawiyya*. Beirut: Dār Ibn Kathīr 1423 AH/2003 CE & Dār al-Jīl, 1411 AH.

Ibn Mājah, Abū ʿAbd Allāh Muḥammad b. Yazīd al-Qazwīnī. *al-Sunan*. Beirut: Dār al-Kutub al-ʿIlmiyya, 1419 AH/1998 CE.

Ibn Rajab al-Ḥanbalī, Zayn al-Dīn ʿAbd al-Raḥmān b. Aḥmad b. Rajab b. al-Ḥasan al-Salāmā al-Baghdādı al-Dimashqī. *Jāmiʿ al-ʿUlūm wa al-Ḥikam fī Sharḥ Khamsīn Ḥadīthan min Jawāmiʿ al-Kalim*. Beirut, Lebanon: Dār al-Maʿrifa, 1408 AH & Muʾassasa al-Risāla, 1417 AH & Egypt: Maṭbaʿa al-Bayālī al-Ḥalabī, 1346 AH.

Kalābādhī, Abū Bakr Muḥammad b. Abī Isḥāq b. Ibrāhīm b. Yaʿqūb, al-. *al-Taʿarruf li Madhhab Ahl al-Taṣawwuf*. Beirut: Dār al-Kutub al-ʿIlmiyya, n.d.

Kāndalwī, Muḥammad Yūsuf b. Muḥammad Ilyās b. Muḥammad

Ismāʿīl, al-. *Ḥayāt al-Ṣaḥāba*. Damascus, Syria: Dār al-Qalam, n.d.

Khaṭīb al-Tabrīzī, Walī al-Dīn Abū ʿAbd Allāh Muḥammad b. ʿAbd Allāh, al-. *Mishkāt al-Maṣābīḥ*. Beirut: Dār al-Kutub al-ʿIlmiyya, 1424 AH/2003 CE.

Khāzin, ʿAlāʾ al-Dīn ʿAlī b. Muḥammad b. Ibrāhīm b. ʿUmar, al-. *Lubāb al-Taʾwīl fī Maʿānī al-Tanzīl*. Beirut: Dār al-Maʿrifa, n.d. & Dār al-Kutub al-ʿIlmiyya, 1415 AH.

Muhājir Makkī, Ḥājī Imdād Allāh. *Taṣfiya al-Qulūb*. Delhi, India: Maṭbaʿ Mujtabāʾī, 1927 CE.

Mullā ʿAlī al-Qārī, Nūr al-Dīn b. Sulṭān Muḥammad al-Hirawī al-Ḥanafī. *Mirqāt al-Mafātīḥ Sharḥ Mishkāt al-Maṣābīḥ*. Mumbai: Aṣaḥḥ al-Maṭābiʿ.

Mundhirī, Abū Muḥammad ʿAbd al-ʿAẓīm b. ʿAbd al-Qawī b. ʿAbd Allāh b. Salāma b. Saʿd, al-. *al-Targhīb wa al-Tarhīb min al-Ḥadīth al-Sharīf*. Beirut, Lebanon: Dār al-Kutub al-ʿIlmiyya, 1417 AH.

Muslim, Ibn al-Ḥajjāj al-Qushayrī. *al-Ṣaḥīḥ*. Beirut: Dār Iḥyāʾ al-Turāth al-ʿArabī, n.d.

Nabhānī, Yūsuf b. Ismāʿīl b. Yūsuf, al-. *Jawāhir al-Biḥār fī Faḍāʾil al-Nabī al-Mukhtār* ﷺ. Beirut, Lebanon: Dār al-Kutub al-ʿIlmiyya, 1419 AH/1998 CE.

Nadwī, Abū al-Ḥasan ʿAlī al-Ḥasanī, al-. *Tazkiya-o-Iḥsān yā Taṣawwuf-o-Sulūk*. Lucknow, India: Lucknow Publishing House, n.d.

Nawawī, Abū Zakariyyā Yaḥyā b. Sharaf b Murrī b. Ḥasan b. Ḥusayn b. Muḥammad b. Jumuʿa b. Ḥizām. *Sharḥ Ṣaḥīḥ Muslim*. Karachi, Pakistan: Qadīmī Kutub Khāna, 1375 AH/1956 CE.

Qāḍī ʿIyāḍ, Abū Faḍl ʿIyāḍ b. Mūsā b. ʿIyāḍ b. ʿAmr b. Mūsā b. ʿIyāḍ b. Muḥammad al-Yaḥṣubī. *al-Shifāʾ bi Taʿrīf Ḥuqūq al-Muṣṭafā* ﷺ. Beirut: Dār al-Kitāb al-ʿArabī, n.d.

Qāḍī Thanāʾ Allāh Pānīpattī. *al-Tafsīr al-Maẓharī*. Pakistan: Maktaba al-Rashīdiyya, 1412 AH & Quetta: Balochistan Book Depot, n.d.

Qasṭallānī, Abū al-ʿAbbās Shihāb al-Dīn Aḥmad b. Muḥammad al-. *al-Mawāhib al-Ladunniyya bi al-Minaḥ al-Muḥammadiyya*. Beirut: al-Maktab al-Islāmī, 1412 AH/1991 CE.

—. *Irshād al-Sārī li Sharḥ Ṣaḥīḥ al-Bukhārī*. Beirut, Lebanon: Dār al-Fikr & Egypt: al-Maṭbaʿa al-Kubrā al-Amīriyya, 7th edition, 1323 AH & Dar al-Fikr, 1304 AH

Rāzī, Fakhr al-Dīn Abū ʿAbd Allāh Muḥammad b. ʿAmr b. al-Ḥasan b. al-Ḥusayn al-Tīmī, al-. *Mafātīḥ al-Ghayb (al-Tafsīr al-Kabīr)*. Beirut, Lebanon: Dār Iḥyāʾ al-Turāth al-ʿArabī, 1420 AH & Tehran, Iran: Dār al-Kutub al-ʿIlmiyya, n.d.

Ṣāwī, Aḥmad b. Muḥammad al-Khalwatī al-Mālikī, al-. *Ḥāshiya ʿalā Tafsīr al-Jalālayn*. Beirut: Dār al-Fikr, 1419 AH/1998 CE & Cairo, Egypt: Maṭbaʿa al-Istiqāma, 1956 CE.

Shabbīr Aḥmad ʿUthmānī, *Ḥāshiya al-Qurʾān* (*Tafsīr ʿUthmānī*), Lahore, Pakistan: Maktaba Raḥmāniyya, n.d.

Shāh ʿAbd al-ʿAzīz, ʿAbd al-ʿAzīz b. Walī Allāh b. ʿAbd al-Raḥīm al-ʿUmarī al-Dihlawī. *Tafsīr al-ʿAzīzī*. Dehli, India: Koh-e-Noor Printing Press, n.d.

Shāh ʿAbd al-Ḥaqq al-Muḥaddith al-Dihlawī, *Maktūbāt* (*Majmūʿat al-Makātib wa al-Rasāʾil*), Karachi, Pakistan: Medina Publishing Company, n.d. [Urdu Translation]

Shāh Ismāʿīl al-Dihlawī. *Ṣirāṭ Mustaqīm*. Deoband, India: Kutub Khāna Ashrafiyya, n.d.

Shāh Walī Allāh al-Dihlawī, Aḥmad b. ʿAbd al-Rahīm b. Wajīh al-Dīn b. Muʿaẓẓam b. Manṣūr. *al-Qawl al-Jamīl*. Lahore, Pakistan: Open Printing Press, 1946 CE.

—. *Anfās al-ʿĀrifīn*. Lahore, Pakistan: Nuri Book Depot & Delhi, India: Maṭbaʿ al-Mujtabāʾī, 1335 AH.

—. *Hamaʿāt*. Hyderabad, Pakistan: Shāh Walī Allāh Academy, n.d

—. *Fuyūḍ al-Ḥaramayn*. Karachi, Pakistan: Qurʾān Maḥall, n.d

—. *al-Intibāh fī Salāsil Awliyāʾ Allāh*. Delhi, India: Maṭbaʿ Burnī, 1344 AH.

Shiblī al-Nuʿmanī. *Sīra al-Nabī* ﷺ. Lahore, Pakistan: Huzayfa Academy, 2000 CE.

Sulamī, Abū ʿAbd al-Raḥmān ʿAbd al-Allāh b. Ḥabīb b. Rabīʿa, al-. *Kitab al-Futuwwa*, n.d.

Ṭabarānī, Abū al-Qāsim Sulaymān b. Aḥmad b. Ayyūb b. Muṭīr al-Lakhmī al-Shāmī, al-. *al-Muʿjam al-Awsaṭ*. Riyadh, Saudi Arabia: Maktaba al-Maʿārif, 1405 AH/1985 CE & Cairo, Egypt: Dār al-Ḥaramayn, 1415 AH.

—. *al-Muʿjam al-Kabīr*. Mosul, Iraq: Maktaba al-Zahrāʾ, 2nd edition, 1404 AH/1983 CE & Cairo, Egypt: Maktaba Ibn Taymiyya, n.d.

Ṭālib Makkī, Muḥammad b. ʿAlī b. ʿAtiyya Abū Ṭālib Makkī. *Qūt al-Qulūb*. Beirut, Lebanon: Dār al-Kutub al-ʿIlmiyya, 2005 CE.

Tirmidhī, Abū ʿĪsā Muḥammad b. ʿĪsā b. Sūra b. Mūsā b. Ḍaḥḥāk al-Sulamī, al-. *al-Sunan*. Beirut: Dār al-Gharb al-Islāmī, 1998 CE.

—. *al-Shamāʾil al-Muḥammadiyya*. Beirut, Lebanon: Muʾassasa al-Kutub al-Thiqāfiyya, 1412 AH.